A Guide to Bible Study

J. W. McGarvey

President of the College of the Bible
Kentucky University

Edited by
Herbert L. Willett
Leader of Bible Study in
the Bethany C.E. Reading Courses

DEWARD
PUBLISHING COMPANY

A Guide to Bible Study
DeWard Publishing Company, Ltd.
P.O. Box 6259, Chillicothe, Ohio 45601
www.dewardpublishing.com

Printed in the United States of America. This DeWard edition was first printed in 2009.

The electronic text was released into the public domain in 1996 as note files for the Online Bible. In this edition, minor changes have been made to the original text. All of these changes are stylistic preferences of the publisher and do not affect the content herein. The vast majority of these changes have been in the style of verse citations (*e.g.*, I Pet. iv: 11 to 1 Pet 4.11) and punctuation (*e.g.*, -- to —). The footnotes and appendixes added by Mr. Willett have been retained in this version.

ISBN: 978-0-9819703-4-9

Contents

Introduction

The indications of a revival of interest in the study of the Bible are numerous and encouraging. They are to be found in the increase of private and devotional reading of the Scriptures, the improvement of lesson helps for the Sunday School, the more conscientious preparation of the lesson among teachers in such schools, the increase of exegetical preaching, the organization of courses of Bible study in young people's societies in nearly all religious bodies, the increase of correspondence Bible work, the creation of Biblical departments in colleges and universities, the establishment of Biblical instruction in connection with state universities, and the organization of clubs and circles for the study of Biblical literature as possessing equal attractiveness with English and other literatures.

The study of the Bible is absolutely necessary to the development of the Christian life. The facts which the Scriptures present are basis of faith in the Christ and in the whole series of providential events which prepared the way for his final disclosure of the life and purposes of God. Only by acquaintance with these facts and the prophetic, devotional, and horatory discourses and meditations to which they gave occasion is one able to understand the Old and New Testaments as the records of our holy faith. The necessity of a daily return to the Scriptures as a means of spiritual nourishment and culture is the more apparent when one notes the fact that a great part of our religious life is made up of activities. This is true of the young people, whose organizations with their various committees and departments lay emphasis on service; it is true of the maturer members of the church, before whom is constantly placed the responsibility for the active ministries to which the gospel calls; and particularly is this true of missionary workers, pastors, teachers and others whose lives are consecrated to Christian service. Where the visible ministries of the church are so largely devoted to the expenditure of spiritual vitality there must be some means of nourishment and recuperation. This is provided in the reading and study of the Word of God, and the atmosphere of prayer in which these privileges should be enjoyed. The nourishment of the Scriptures is as necessary to the spiritual life as that of food to the body.

This hand-book is designed to afford suggestion and assistance to those who desire a fuller and more accurate knowledge of the Bible. It gives a brief summary of facts regarding the making and the purpose of the Bible; its chief divisions; short sketches of the various books, serving as introductions to their study; and various other material of an interesting and helpful sort to the reader and student of the Bible. The book has its purposes and its limitations. The former has been noted. The latter was set by the desire to put all the material into such a brief and convenient form that the little volume could be in reality what its name implies, a hand-book, constantly kept at hand for reference and suggestion.

A few suggestions as to a method of Bible reading and study may be found profitable.

1. Use the Revised Version of the Bible if possible. It is much superior to the Authorized or King James Version, not only because of its better interpretation of particular words and passages, but because the translators of 1881–1884 availed themselves of many principles of interpretation unknown to those of 1611. The Revised Version is not perfect, but it is a long advance over its predecessor and is gradually coming to take its place with those who desire to possess the best version of the Scriptures. There may be a feeling of reluctance on the part of those who have long used the older translation at the thought of giving up its familiar phrases, but one who has before him the most of his career as a Bible student cannot afford to deprive himself of the advantages resulting from the used of the Revised Version.

2. The Bible should be studied with a good map at hand for constant reference showing the localities, which were the scenes of the events recorded. If possible some good work on Biblical Geography should be at hand. One is never able so thoroughly to realize any event of which the Bible speaks, *i.e.,* to make it real to himself, as when he visits the spot in person, or by the assistance of good description of the place, or possesses even a map to show its location and relation to other localities. Almost any good edition of the Bible, either of the Authorized or the Revised Version, contains a set of maps. They should be constantly used till the student is thoroughly acquainted with Biblical localities.

3. Some general plan of Biblical chronology should be used for frequent reference. No system thus far devised is altogether satisfactory, because the writers of the Bible were not particularly concerned about dates and give them usually in relation to other events, so that one is often able only to approximate the real time of an event. The chronology employed in the margin of the Authorized Version was that of Archbishop Ussher, and has been found quite unsatisfactory in many particulars as judged by light thrown, especially on Old Testament events, by recent researches among the records of nations with which Israel came into contact. An outline chronology of the leading periods and events in the Biblical history is given in the appendix to this handbook. Exactness of date is neither possible nor necessary in many cases, but a plan of dates relatively correct should be mastered by every student.

4. The gradual character of the Biblical revelation should be firmly impressed in the beginning of any study of the Scriptures. The divine purposes were disclosed only as they could be understood. A nation was chosen to be the channel of that revelation, and its education was to that end; not for its own sake, but for the world. The Old Testament is the record of that national discipline. Not everything could be taught at once, but only step by step could advance be made. Progress is seen through the whole of the Old Testament dispensation in the disclosure of truth and its embodiment in character, in preparation for the appearance of the

Christ. The New Testament is the record of his manifestation to the world; of the gradual spread of the Gospel, and of the helps to the progressive realization of the Christian life.

5. The student should seek such familiarity with the books of the Bible that their names, groupings and contents can be instantly recalled. These items are all important. The knowledge of the names of the books of the Bible in their order is indispensable and easily acquired. To assist in the possession of this knowledge, and to render it still more accurate and detailed, it should be remembered that the Old Testament books fall into three groups, which, speaking in general terms, may be called (I) historical, 17; (II) poetical, 5; (III) prophetic, 17; 39 in all. In the New Testament there are also three groups; (I) historical, the Gospels and Acts, 5; (II) didactic, the Epistles, 21; (III) apocalyptic, Revelation, 1; 27 in all, a total of 66 in the Bible. Then in the study of a particular book its plan and contents may be secured. The ability to "think through" a book, *i.e.,* to recall the general line of through its chapters, is the only knowledge that can satisfy the real Bible student.

6. The memorizing of portions of Scripture is a practice that should be followed, and whose results will be most satisfactory both as a means of a better understanding of the Bible and as aids to the religious life. The habit of committing to memory a passage of Scripture daily is easily acquired, and presently the mind is stored with the most precious utterances of the ages.

7. References in the New Testament to passages in the Old Testament should be carefully searched out, and incidents narrated in different places should be compared. This may be done with the aid of the references found in the Authorized Version, but unfortunately the system there adopted often runs to fantastic lengths, references being sometimes given on the basis of quite superficial resemblance. One's own references, neatly set down on the margins of his Bible in the light of careful study, will always be found the most helpful.

8. In short, the ability to do one's own study and come upon one's own results is the goal of all methods. Notes of work done should

be made. Condensations and paraphrases of passages may be made with profit. "A lead pencil is the best of all commentators." A notebook should be in constant use. Results may be written on the margin of the Bible page in ink. Many systems of "Bible marking" have been devised. Few are of any value except to those who devise them; but any good method of preserving results, worked out by the student himself, will prove of value.

9. The use of any helps that may be within reach is advisable. But they should be used as *helps,* and not usurp the place of the Bible itself. After all, it is the Bible we are to study, and no mere study of books can compensate for a failure to study first and constantly the Book.

10. The use to be made of this hand-book will suggest itself to every student. In taking up the study of any book, read that book carefully. Then read the material on that book in the following pages. After this read the material on the other books of the same group, that the surroundings of the particular book may be obtained. From these readings a knowledge of its date, or that of its events, will be secured, which may be supplemented by the chronological material furnished in the appendix. Then read the book through at a single sitting if possible, to get its leading ideas. After this make an outline of its contents, and lastly turn to the questions on the book in the appendix and write out full answers to them. The results of such a use of this little book will render it of value to every one so using it, and will amply justify its preparation.

Herbert L. Willett

1. Definitions

The word Bible is derived from the Greek word *biblos*, which means *book*. Used as a title it means *The* Book, so called by the way of pre-eminence. This title is not found in the Bible itself; but it came into use among believers after the Bible was completed.

The titles, *Old Testament* and *New Testament*, also came into use after the completion of the Bible. The books which pass under the latter title contain a new covenant which God made with men, while those under the former contain the old covenant which he made with Israel at Mount Sinai (Heb 8.6–13; Jer 31.31–34). In the Latin Bible the word for covenant is translated *Testamentum;* and from this, at a time when the Latin Bible was the most read in Europe, the title *Testament* came into its present use.

The title *Scriptures,* sometimes with the prefix Holy, is a New Testament title for the books of the Old Testament. In 2 Peter 3.16 it is also applied by implication to the Epistles of Paul; and it some came into use as a title for the whole Bible. The word means writings, and in its first sense it could be applied to any writings; but as the expression, The Book, came to mean one particular book, so the expression, The Scriptures, came to mean *The* Writings in the Bible. When the term Holy is prefixed, this still further distinguishes these writings.

The apostles Paul and Peter both use the title "Oracles of God," for the Old Testament books, and Stephen calls them "The Living Oracles" (Rom 3.2; Heb 5.12; 1 Pet 4.11; Acts 7.38). By oracles is meant utterances of God; and these books were so called, because they contain utterances of God through inspired men. They are called living oracles; because of their abiding power in contrast with the deadness of heathen oracles. But if the Old Testament books are worthy of this title, still more are those of the New Testament; and consequently Papias, a Christian writer of the second century, applies it to Matthew's book, saying, "Matthew wrote the Oracles." This is especially true of Matthew, because more than half of his book is composed of speeches made by Jesus. It is entirely proper then to speak of the whole Bible as The Oracles of God, or The Living Oracles.

2. Divisions of the Old Testament

Every intelligent person knows that the Bible is not one continuous book, but it is made up of a number of books, differing from one another in subject matter and literary form. Some are books of history, some of prophecy, some of precept or doctrine, and some of poetry. They are also distinguished with reference to the time in which they were written, and the purposes which they were intended to serve. In order to read them intelligibly it is necessary to take notice of all these distinctions.

The first five books (let the reader here commit their names to memory if he has not already done so), are commonly grouped under the title, The Pentateuch,[1] a Greek word which means a five-fold book.

Next we have twelve historical books, containing a connected history of Israel from the death of Moses to the restoration after the Babylonian captivity. The reader should commit their names to memory. Two of these, First and Second Chronicles, repeat large portions of the history given in other books, but they also furnish much additional information.

In the middle of our Bible, next after the books last mentioned, we find five books, mostly poetry (commit their names to memory), which are placed without regard to their time of composition. In our Lord's classification of the Old Testament as "the law, the prophets and the psalms," they are included under the latter title, because the book of Psalms was the best known

---

[1] Another arrangement includes in one group the first six books. This group, Genesis to Joshua, is usually called the Hexateuch. —W.

of the five. It is now quite common among scholars to include Job, Proverbs, and Ecclesiastes under the title, *Wisdom Literature*, because of the prominence given in them about wisdom and folly. These five books are grouped together because a likeness in subject matter and literary form distinguishes them from the others. It should be observed that the arrangement of the books in the Bible is the work of uninspired editors and publishers, and not of the inspired authors.

The last division of all is composed of seventeen books which are styled prophetical (commit their names to memory). These, like the preceding division, are grouped together, because of their likeness in subject matter. Some of them were written after the Babylonian exile, and some long before it. They follow one another on the pages of the Bible without regard to the order of time. Nearly every one indicates in the opening verses the time of its composition by giving the names of the kings under whom its author lived and prophesied.

This classification of the books of the Old Testament, if remembered, as it must be by all who wish to become proficient in Scripture knowledge, will enable the student at any time to readily turn to the part he wishes to read, whether law, history, poetry, or prophecy. Every part has its own peculiar value both for instruction and edification; and no part should be neglected.

3. The Original Text and Its Preservation

The books of the Old Testament were all written, with unimportant exceptions to be mentioned hereafter, in the Hebrew tongue, which was the native tongue of the Hebrew nation. As the earliest of them were written more than three thousand years ago, and the latest more than two thousand years ago, it is proper to inquire, what assurance we have that our present books are the same as those in the original collection, and that they contain the same words. To give a full answer to these questions would require a whole volume as large as this, but can give the principal facts in a few lines.

During the period from the first writing of the books till the invention of printing, all copies were made with the pen, and it has been found impracticable to copy books in this way without making some mistakes. These occur chiefly in the spelling of words, and in the omission or insertion of words not essential to the meaning of a sentence; but a few occurred which affect the sense, and which sometimes introduce contradictions of a book with itself, or with another book. Especially is this last the case with names and numbers, in which the copyist had no train of thought to guide him. This accounts for the discrepancies in numbers which every thoughtful reader has noticed between certain passages in Chronicles and the corresponding passages in the books of Samuel and Kings.

After this process had continued until the error of copyists at-

tracted the serious attention of Jewish scholars, a company of them
drew up some very stringent rules to prevent such errors in the future. They counted the number of words in every book by sections,
and marked the middle word of every section. Then they required
every copyist, when he had copied the middle word, to count back
and see if he had the right number of words. If he had, there
was good assurance that he had omitted none and added none.
If he had not, the part written was to be thrown away and a new
copy made. These rules were adopted in the second century after
Christ, and from that time forward no errors worth considering
crept into the Hebrew Scriptures. When printing was invented,
which was in the year 1448, and the Hebrew Old Testament was
published in this form, which was in 1477, no more copies were
written by hand, and the making of mistakes by copying came to
an end; for when the types for a book are once set up correctly, all
copies printed from them are precisely alike.

The question whether any of the original books have been lost,
or others added, is settled by the fact that a Greek translation of
the Old Testament was made, beginning in the year 280 before
Christ, which has come down to our day, and it contains the same
books. There can be no reasonable doubt, therefore, that we now
have the Old Testament substantially the same as when its several
books were originally written.

4. Outline of the Pentateuch

Genesis, Exodus, Leviticus, Numbers, Deuteronomy

a. *Genesis.* It is a singular fact that many of the titles of the Hebrew books are Greek words. This grew out of the circumstance that the ancient Hebrews were not accustomed to giving titles to their books, but when they were translated into Greek, the translators, according to the custom in that language, gave titles to them. The title Genesis (creation) was given to the first book, because it begins with an account of creation.

Starting with a brief account of creation, the first general division of this book gives a very few incidents in the history of our race till the birth of Abraham. This division includes the first eleven chapters. The events which it records are chiefly connected with the increasing wickedness of men by which God was constrained to destroy all except Noah's family in the waters of a flood. After the account of the flood there follows an extremely brief account of the re-peopling of the earth by the descendants of Noah, and of their unwilling dispersion into different communities through the confusion of tongues. In the course of this brief record, we find two genealogies—that of Noah, which is traced back to Adam, and that of Abraham, which is traced back to Noah; and by means of the two we trace back to Adam the ancestry of Abraham. At the close of chapter eleven the narrative changes from a general history of men, to a biography of a single man. This biography of one man, who lived only one hundred and seventy-five years, occupies one and a half times as much space as the previous history of all men. We thus discover that the author's main theme thus far is his account of Abraham, and that the preceding portion was tended chiefly as an introduction to this.

The story of Abraham contains much that is interesting and edifying; and it should be studied in connection with the many references to it in the New Testament, which are all pointed out on the margin of any good reference Bible; but the chief interest in it to the mind of the author of Genesis, seems to be centered upon certain promises made to him by God. One was, that he would give to him and his seed the land of Canaan, in which he was then living as a stranger; another was, that his posterity should be as numerous as the stars of heaven, or the sands in the seashore; and another, that in him and in his seed should all the nations of the earth be blessed. In connection with the second of these, he was commanded to circumcise all the males born in his house, or bought with his money, and was told that this ordinance should be observed by his posterity forever. This rite served to distinguish his posterity among men, so that it might be seen in subsequent generations that God's promise was kept. These promises necessarily looked forward, and the author kept them in mind as he wrote the remainder of this and the other books of the Pentateuch.

In connection with the first of these promises, God told Abraham that before his seed should possess the promised land, they should be in bondage in a foreign land four hundred years, but should come out a great nation, and then take possession of Canaan. The rest of the book is taken up with the various fortunes of his descendants, many of which are thrillingly interesting, till his grandson Jacob, with a family of sixty-eight living descendants, is led by a mysterious chain of providences to take up his abode in Egypt, preparatory to the fulfillment of the last mentioned prediction. The book closes with the death of Joseph, the eleventh son of Jacob, through whose instrumentality the family had been brought into Egypt, and who in dying spoke of the promised return to Canaan, and gave his brethren charge to carry his bones with them for final burial in that land.

A glance backward will now show the reader that the main

design of the author of Genesis was to give the history of Abraham's family down to the migration into Egypt; that the previous account of the whole world was preparatory to this; and all this was preparatory to an account yet to be given of the fulfillment of predictions and promises made to Abraham.

We find that the author goes over in this short book nearly 2,500 years of the world's history; and yet the book, if printed by itself, would be only a small pamphlet.

b. *Exodus.* This book is called Exodus (going out), because a prominent event in it is the departure of Israel out of Egypt. The name, like Genesis, is Greek. The book is divided into three distinct parts. The first traces the steps by which the Hebrews, whose coming into Egypt was warmly welcomed by the king, were finally brought into bondage; and those by which, under the leadership of Moses, they were delivered after a residence in that land of four hundred and thirty years. Nearly the whole world had at that time fallen into idolatry; and the method which God chose for the deliverance of Israel was also intended to make himself once more known to the Egyptians and the surrounding nations, while it also made him much better known to his own people. Moses was the first missionary to the heathen. The second part shows the wonderful way in which God sustained the people in the wilderness; how he led them to Mt. Sinai; and how he there entered into a covenant with them, and gave them a set of laws, civil and religious, to govern them as a nation. The third part describes a sanctuary, or place of worship which he caused them to erect, and which could be easily moved with them through all of their subsequent journeys. By these events was fulfilled the promise to Abraham, "That nation whom they shall serve, will I judge; and afterward shall they come out with great substance"; for the fulfillment of the various promises to Abraham runs like a thread through all the subsequent history of his people.

c. *Leviticus.* This book is filled with a set of laws, regulating the sacrifices and purifications which were connected with the worship at the sanctuary, together with a few ethical precepts intended to cultivate holiness and righteousness among the people. It is because these ceremonies were to be administered by the priests the sons of Aaron and other Levites, that the book was named by the Greek translators, Leviticus.

d. *Numbers.* This name was given from the circumstance that the numbering of Israel twice by the command of God is recorded in it, the first numbering near the beginning, and the second near the close. The book gives an account of the journeyings and other experiences of Israel, during the period of about thirty-eight years, in which they were wandering from Mt. Sinai to the eastern bank of the river Jordan, whence they finally crossed over into Canaan. Many of their experiences were of the most thrilling character, rendering this a most interesting book. In the course of these events many new laws were given, God having reserved these to be given in connection with events which seemed to call for them, and to this make the enactment of them more impressive than it otherwise could be. It was a time of wonderful divine discipline, in the course of which the whole generation of grown persons who crossed the Red Sea perished, with the exception of two, and a new generation was brought up under the training of the Lord. These could be expected to serve God in their new home more faithfully than their fathers would have done. Even Moses and Aaron were among those who died in the wilderness. God had now, according to the promise to Abraham, brought them out of their bondage in Egypt and judged that nation.

e. *Deuteronomy.* This name means *the second law.* It was given because the Greek translators found in it a repetition of some laws previously given, and the enactment of some new laws. The main body of the book is made up of three discourses delivered by Moses in the plain of Moab over against Jericho, beginning on the first day of the eleventh month of the fortieth year, or just two and a half months before the close of forty years since the start out of Egypt (1.3). The first discourse, beginning with 1.6, and closing with 4.40, would be called, in our modern style, a historical sermon; for it consists in a rehearsal of all the leading events of the previous forty years, with practical lessons drawn from them, and exhortations based on them. It is an admirable specimen of that kind of preaching, and it should be studied as such by the preachers of the present day.

The discourse is followed by a brief statement about the cities of refuge east of the Jordan, and this by a kind of introduction to the second discourse. The second discourse begins with chapter fifth, and closes with chapter twenty-sixth. In it Moses rehearses many of the laws which had been given in the previous years of the wanderings, beginning with the ten commandments; adds a few new statutes; and warmly exhorts the people to keep them all and to teach them diligently to their children. In this discourse, much more than in any other part of the Pentateuch, there is a constant appeal to the love of God as the one great motive to obedience; and the ground of that love is pointed out repeatedly in the unexampled goodness of God toward Israel.

The third discourse, beginning with the twenty-seventh chapter and closing with the thirtieth, is prophetical; proclaiming a long and fearful list of curses which would befall the people if they should depart from the service of Jehovah, and of the blessings if they should be faithful to him.

The last four chapters are occupied with the announcement of the approaching death of Moses; a formal charge to Joshua as his successor; a statement about his committing the law to writing and charging the Levites with its preservation; two poems; an account of his death; and some comments by a later writer on his career.

These discourses and poems, like the exhortation which ends a long sermon, bring the Pentateuch to a most fitting conclusion; for they gather up and concentrate upon the heart of the reader all the moral power of the eventful history from Adam down, by way of exalting the name of Jehovah and filling the hearts of his people with gratitude. Especially was this so with the Israelites who saw in the past the unfolding of God's gracious purposes toward them as declared in his promises to their father Abraham. When Moses disappeared from among them he left them with nothing but the narrow channel of the Jordan between them and the land of promise to which God had now, after dreary centuries, brought them in exact fulfillment of his word. The teaching of that fulfillment constitutes the unity of the Pentateuch.

The time covered by the Pentateuch, according to the figures given on its pages, is 2,760 years. This is nearly twice as much time as is covered by all the rest of the Bible.

5. Israel's History from the Death of Moses to that of David

Joshua, Judges, Ruth, First Samuel, Second Samuel

While the twelve historical books which follow the Pentateuch give us, as we have said in a former chapter, an almost continuous history down to the close of the Old Testament period, the study of this history is facilitated by considering it according to the several distinct periods into which it naturally divides itself. We chose first, as best suiting our present purpose, the one named at the head of this chapter, and we shall set it forth by giving outlines of the several books in which the history is found.

a. *Joshua.* This book is so called, not because Joshua wrote it, although it is possible that he did so, but because it is he who figures most conspicuously in the transactions which it records.

The book is divided into three distinct parts. The first, beginning where the Pentateuch left off with Israel on the east bank of the Jordan, describes their miraculous passage of the swollen river, and their conquests, in two great campaigns, of the whole land of Canaan, with the exception of a few tribes who were so weakened as not to hinder the settlement of the country by the Hebrews. This brought to a final fulfillment the promise to Abraham that God would give him this land as an inheritance for his posterity. This part includes the first twelve chapters.

The second part, including chapters thirteen to twenty-two, gives the location of the several tribes, chiefly by naming the cities within their respective lots. These chapters might be called the Biblical Geography of Palestine. The student should here take up a good map and learn the location of every tribe, and of all the principal cities, mountains, plains, and waters. The closing part, twenty-third and twenty-fourth chapters, is occupied with two farewell addresses delivered by Joshua, one of the civil office-holders of all Israel, and the other to a mass meeting of the whole people, and with a very brief account of the death and burial of Joshua, and of Eleazer the priest. It also mentions the burial of the bones, or mummy, of Joseph, which had been brought out of Egypt. Israel is now settled as a nation in the promised land, and the promises respecting that land which had been made to Abraham and repeated to Isaac and Jacob, are fulfilled.

b. *Judges.* This book opens with an account of the separate actions of the several tribes in driving out the Canaanites who were left in their territories after the death of Joshua, though it also contains a repetition of one conquest by the tribe of Judah which had been achieved before Joshua died. Then, in a kind of preface, the author occupies the rest of the first two chapters with a brief statement of the alternate apostasies and deliverances which make up the history in the rest of the book. These two chapters may be styled Part First. Then follows Part Second, chapters three to sixteen, in which sometimes one tribe and sometimes many fall into idolatry; are subdued or greatly harassed by their enemies until they repent and call upon God; are then delivered under the leadership of a Judge raised up by the Lord for the purpose; are kept in the fear of God until the Judge dies, when the same round of events is repeated to the twelfth time. There was no central government; but to answer the purposes of such when necessity required, Judges were providentially raised up and the accounts which we have of them here gave the name Judges to this book.

The third part of the book, chapters seventeen to twenty-one, gives two incidents which have been passed over by the writer to avoid an interruption of the main thread of the history. The one shows how an idolatrous worship which was set up at Dan, and continued there for several centuries, was first inaugurated; and the other shows how the whole nation came together at an early day to punish a great crime, when the city and the tribe within which it had been committed refused to do so.

The general design of the book of Judges seems to be to exhibit the working of both civil and religious law during the first three or four hundred years of Israel's experiences under it. In both respects there had been a comparative failure, as is also true in the history of every nation both ancient and modern; but under this divine discipline many men and women of eminent virtues were developed.

c. *Ruth.* The romantic incidents of this beautiful story occurred while the Judges ruled in Israel (1.1), and one of its purposes, the only one that appears till the closing paragraph brings out another, is to present a better phase of life under the Judges than we find in the book of Judges. This it does in a most charming manner. But at the close we ascertain that it was also intended to show that a woman of Moab was among the material ancestors of David, and to trace the interesting circumstances by which this was brought about. It could scarcely have been written before the reign of David; for it was David's reign that gave public interest to his genealogy.

d. *First Samuel.* This book begins with the last of the Judges and closes with the death of the first king. It contains, therefore, an account of the change in the form of government. It shows how the political and religious degeneration, which had been going on in the latter part of the rule of the Judges, sank to its lowest point in the moral corruption of the priesthood, when the people came to abhor the sacrifices of Jehovah on account of the wickedness of the priests who offered them. It shows also that political degradation reached its lowest point with the degradation of religion; and that then the ark of the covenant, which was the symbol of God's presence with Israel, was captured and taken away by their old enemies, the Philistines. This introduced an irregularity in the worship on the part of those who continued to serve God, and it led to a demand on the part of the people for a king to rule over them. This demand was treated as a sin of the people, because it was their own sins, and not an inherent defect in the form of government which God had given them, that brought about the failure. Nevertheless, God had foreseen this result, and had provided beforehand for it, and consequently he gave them a king in the person of Saul the son of Kish. In the meantime the prophet Samuel had brought about a great religious reformation among the people, and if Saul had proved to be a faithful servant of God, the affairs of the whole nation would in every way have been greatly improved. But though Saul was a skillful warrior, and fought many victorious battles, he turned away from God in many things, and his career ended in death on the battlefield. His reign closed, as did the rule of the Judges, in a defeat which left the people once more in subjection to the Philistines, once more illustrating the rule that righteousness exalteth a nation, while sin is a disgrace to any people. This is the lesson most strikingly taught by this portion of Israel's history. The book also shows how God prepared another man in the person of David to take the place of Saul, and to reign more worthily than he did. It also strikingly exhibits the career of the greatest prophet who had thus far appeared in Israel since the days of Moses; for Samuel was not only an eminently good man, but he was also a successful ruler, and even a king-maker, seeing that under God he selected and anointed as kings both Saul and David; and until his death, which was mourned by the whole nation, both these men and all the people looked to him for counsel in every great crisis. From this time forward the special officers raised up from time to time to represent God are prophets, as under the preceding period they had been Judges.

e. *Second Samuel.* In the Hebrew Bible our two books of Samuel are but one; and in the English the history goes on from the one into the other without a break. The division was made for convenience in making references and in finding particular passages. Neither of them bears the name Samuel because Samuel wrote it;

but because he figured so largely in starting the course of events which they record. He died before the events in First Samuel had all transpired. The present book opens with David's accession to the throne, first over Judah, and after a seven-years war, over all Israel. The history had now reached the point at which another of the ancient promises of God began to be fulfilled; for it was promised to Jacob, "A nation and a company of nations shall be of thee, and kings shall come out of thy loins"; and Judah had been pointed out as the son of Jacob through whom this promise should be fulfilled; for in Jacob's dying prophecy about his sons he had said, "The sceptre shall not depart from Judah till Shiloh[1] come." In fulfillment of this promise, David, a descendant of Judah by the genealogy recorded in the book of Ruth, was now a reigning king, and his posterity were to reign in succession after him. To show this was a leading design of the book. It also shows, by the career of David, even more strikingly than was seen in the career of Saul, that prosperity attends a king while he serves God, and adversity comes with disobedience; for this book, from the point at which it finds David on the throne, is divided into two very distinct parts, which may be styled, The Prosperous Part of David's Reign (chs 5–10) and David's Adversity (chs 12–24). The two parts are separated by the great sin which has been associated with David's name from the day it was exposed until now. The same great lesson is taught in the careers of many men prominently connected with David. This makes the second book of Samuel one of the most profitable for reading and reflection of all the books of the Old Testament.

This book also brings out the fact that the reign of David was a period of decided literary activity in Israel, for it publishes several of David's poems, and it connects the history with the contents of the book of Psalms, many of the poems in which were composed by him. We learn also from the book of Chronicles, that the prophets Samuel, Nathan and Gad, were authors of works which

---

[1]The word rendered "Shiloh" is obscure. It may mean "Peace." Somewhat better renderings are "Till he come to Shiloh" (Josh 18.1) or "Till he to whom it belongs shall come." —W.

jointly included all the acts of David, "first and last" (1 Chron 29.29–30). It is highly probable that at this period the books of Ruth and Judges, and much of the book of Samuel were written. The book of Jasher too, which is mentioned only twice, once to state that it contained an account of Joshua's command to the sun and moon to stand still, and once to say that David's lamentation over the death of Saul was written in it, was probably written at this time, seeing that it is not mentioned in connection with any later event. It was evidently a book of great value and authority, though it was allowed afterward to perish.

During David's reign the reader should not fail to observe that God's chosen messengers to declare his will from time to time, in matters both of government and of morals, continued to exercise authority even over the king. This was especially true of Nathan and Gad, of whom we know little besides this.

6. The Reign of Solomon and the Divisions of the Kingdom

The subject of this chapter is set forth in the first twelve chapters of First Kings, and the first ten chapters of Second Chronicles. The account begins by showing that Solomon came near losing the throne and his life through a conspiracy of his older brother Adonijah, who, being the oldest living son of David, claimed the right to the throne, and was supported in this claim by such men as Joab and the high priest Abiathar. This conspiracy was undertaken before David's death, and he was supposed to be so decrepit that he could not interfere. But he was aroused to activity by the combined efforts of the prophet Nathan and the mother of Solomon, and the conspiracy was nipped in the bud by the immediate anointing of Solomon.

The young king's choice of wisdom, when God gave him his choice as to what should be given him, is the key-note of the earlier part of his reign, and it brings into startling contrast the apostasy which characterized the last few years of his life. The chief event of his reign is the erection of the temple which replaced the old Tent of Meeting erected by Moses. This brought to an end, at least among the faithful, the irregular worship that had prevailed ever since the capture of the ark by the Philistines, and it enabled the priests to subsequently conduct the services according to all the provision of the law.

After building the temple, and also a magnificent palace for himself, Solomon proceeded to inaugurate a complete system of fortification at strategic points in his kingdom, so that one or more of these would confront an enemy from whatever point he might attempt to march an invading army toward Jerusalem. It was probably this wise precaution, together with an alliance by marriage with the reigning king of Egypt, that preserved his kingdom in peace throughout his long reign of forty years.

The literary activity which had sprung into being in the reign of David, reached its culmination in that of Solomon. He himself took the lead in it, by writing many poems and proverbs, and by discoursing on nearly all subjects which are now grouped under the general title of Natural History. Biographical writing was also cultivated, and the prophets, Nathan, Ahijah and Iddo are mentioned as writers of this class.

Solomon was the first king of Israel to engage in commerce, and especially in the mining of the precious metals, which he found in rich abundance in a region called Ophir, whose mines were soon exhausted so that the place itself has ceased to be known. These enterprises brought him in contact with the outside world, and he became by far the most famous king who at any time reigned in Israel. His wealth bred a fondness for magnificence, and this led him to multiply wives, horses and chariots, and these again to complicity with the worship of idols.

The prosperity of the kingdom under Solomon, as it was very largely secured by oppressive levies upon the working classes of his subjects, wrought out its own destruction, as the historian proceeds to relate after Solomon's death. The people petitioned his son and successor to lessen the burdens imposed by the father; he answered them contemptuously, and ten of the tribes, under the leadership of Jeroboam, a bold man of the tribe of Ephraim, revolted and set up a rival kingdom. Once more was Israel taught that national prosperity was to be secured only by strict adherence to the will of God.[1]

---

[1] The conduct of Ahijah the Prophet (1 Kgs 11.29–35) in encouraging Jeroboam to revolt, indicates the feeling on the part of the prophets that the interests of true religion required a simpler form of national life than the splendors of Solomon's reign encouraged. —W.

7. The Two Kingdoms

1 Kings 1–12; 2 Chronicles 1–12: The First Period of Hostility, The Period of Reconciliation, The Second Period of Hostility

From the division of the kingdom till the downfall of that of the ten tribes, called the kingdom of Israel, or the northern kingdom, while the other was the kingdom of Judah, or the southern kingdom, the author of the book of Kings treats their history alternately, while the Chronicler confines himself to the latter, except when the two come in contact.

We should study this part of the history under the subdivisions into which it is naturally divided, and we must take into view the writings of the prophets as they come into contact with the history; for the latter constitute a very important part of the history of the times, and without them the narrative in Kings and Chronicles could be but imperfectly understood.

This portion of the history divides itself into three distinct parts which we shall consider separately. They are first, a period of hostility between the two kingdoms; second, a period of friendly alliance; and third, a second period of hostility.

1. *The First Period of Hostility.* This period began with the division of the kingdom, and closed with an alliance between kings Ahab and Jehoshaphat, and it lasted about 78 years. At the beginning of this period Jeroboam established the worship of Jehovah under the image of golden calves at Bethel and Dan; ordained an annual festival at the former place, and made it unlawful for his subjects to go to Jerusalem to worship as the law of Moses required. The author of the book of Kings is careful to trace the continuance of this unlawful worship in the reigns of subsequent kings of Israel, and the evil consequences of it are plainly seen in the course of events. Within about fifty years four different dynasties came to the throne, each exterminating the male offspring of the predecessor, and each being pronounced more wicked than those that had gone before. Finally the religious degradation reached such a point that to the calf-worship inaugurated by Jeroboam was added the almost universal worship of Baal. In this crisis the greatest of all the prophets who have left no writings behind them, Elijah the Tishbite, appeared like a sudden thunderstorm on the scene, and gave a staggering blows to this pernicious system.

In the meantime, the kingdom of Judah had progressed more satisfactorily. Adhering to the true God, and maintaining his worship according to the law, only four kings had come to the throne when the seventh began to reign in Israel. During a temporary apostasy of the people under Rehoboam, the country was overrun by an Egyptian army, and a heavy tribute was paid to get rid of it; but a return to the Lord brought a return to prosperity, and Jehoshaphat was reigning righteously over Judah while Ahab was in the midst of the wickedest reign that had been known in Israel.

2. *The Period of Reconciliation.* The two kingdoms so long hostile now became reconciled by the marriage of Ahab's daughter Athaliah to Jehoram the son and heir of Jehoshaphat. The alliance emboldened Ahab to a military enterprise which he had not dared to undertake alone, and which resulted in the defeat of his army and the loss of his life. The whole story of his reign is full of instruction and warning. Jehoshaphat was rebuked by a messenger from God for helping those who were the enemies of God; but the friendly relations between his kingdom and that of Israel continued until the former reaped much bitter fruit therefrom. Athaliah proved a scourge to Judah, and in the third generation of Jehoshaphat's descendants she attempted the extermination of the royal family. She came so near succeeding that only one infant was left to perpetuate the family of David, and to make possible the divine promise that he should never lack a son to sit upon his throne. This infant was saved at the sacrifice of Athaliah's own execrable life, and then came to an end the alliance between Israel and Judah which had proved a continuous disaster to the latter.

While such was the course of history in Judah, Israel had fared no better. Ahab's son and successor, Ahaziah, reigned only two years. He made a feeble effort to revive Baal worship, and he also committed the fatal sin of his life by sending messengers to Baal-zebub, the god of Ekron, to inquire of him the result of an injury which he had received from a fall. Dying without a son, he was succeeded by his brother Jehoram, in whose reign the career of Elijah came to a glorious end, and the brilliant career of Elisha kept alive to some extent the fear of God among the people. More than once he saved the kingdom from subjugation by Benhadad the powerful king of Syria. Jehoram's career ended in the extermination of the whole offspring of Ahab by the hand of Jehu.

That the two great prophets, Elijah and Elisha, were sent to the more wicked of the two kingdoms, though a matter of surprise at first thought, was the very thing to be expected; for their mission was to rebuke sin, and where sin most abounded was their proper field of activity. By checking Baal-worship in the larger kingdom, where it originated, they brought it to a speedier end in the smaller kingdom to which it had spread.

3. *The Second Period of Hostility.* After the extermination of the house of Ahab in Israel, and the death of Athaliah in Judah, there was no more co-operation between the two kingdoms; but instead there were frequent wars as of old. The house of Jehu held the throne in the north longer than any other, and under Jeroboam II the kingdom reached its greatest power and prosperity since the days of Solomon. This king, by the prophetic guidance of the prophet Jonah, subdued the kingdom of Syria which had long oppressed his nation, and extended his dominions to the Euphrates, which was the northern boundary of the kingdom of David. The incidents recorded in the book of Jonah belong to this reign.

It was in this reign, which was a long one, that the prophets Hosea and Amos uttered the prophecies which we find in their books. It is necessary to study these, in order to fully understand the condition of the people at the time; for while the account in the historical book of Kings touches upon political and military affairs, and this very slightly, the two prophets speak to the people of their sins; and in doing so they bring to light a state of irreligion and immorality in the midst of secular prosperity, which fills the reader with horror, and which is yet but the legitimate result of the experiences through which the ten tribes had passed since the division of the kingdom. It is also worthy of special notice that they predicted the downfall and ruin of the kingdom at the very time when, according to all human foresight, there was less prospect of such a disaster than at any previous period in its history.

After the fall of the house of Jehu, which occurred in six months after the death of Jeroboam II, the kingdom hastened rapidly to the doom predicted for it by Hosea and Amos. A succession of five kings came to the throne in thirty-two years, all of whom but one were assassinated by their successors. In their rivalries they hired three successive kings of Assyria to interfere in their affairs, thus fairly inviting the rulers of that great Empire to come at last, as they did, and take the whole kingdom into captivity. Finally in the ninth year of the last of these assassins, Hoshea, the end came as described in the seventeenth chapter of 2 Kings.

While Israel was thus going the downward road to destruction, Judah, having recovered somewhat from the damaging effects of the alliance with the house of Ahab, passed through a happier career, though not without some severe rebukes from the two prophets who were specially sent to Israel. Of the six kings who reigned during the time of the ten in Israel, two were faithful to God and his law, while three were unfaithful in many things, but far less so than the kings of Israel.

The last of these good kings, Hezekiah, was in the sixth year of his reign when Israel was carried captive.

The whole period of the separate existence of the two kingdoms, counted by adding together the reigns of the kings and making a proper reduction for the peculiar Hebrew method of counting, in 354 years, and the modern date of captivity of Israel is BC 721.

8. The Kingdom of Judah Continued

2 Kings 18–25; 2 Chronicles 29–36

This history of the kingdom of Judah, from the fall of Israel to its own fall, is found in 2 Kings, from the eighteenth chapter to the close, and in 2 Chronicles, from chapter twenty-nine to the close. Some of it is also found in the books of the prophets who wrote during that period, especially in those of Isaiah and Jeremiah. The time included was about 130 years, covering the reigns of eight kings. Of these two reigned only three months each, and one only two years. The first, Hezekiah, was a good king, the best who had reigned since the division of the kingdom. He was preceded, however, by two kings, Jotham and Ahaz, who were very wicked, and under their evil influence the people had become very corrupt. It was therefore with great difficulty that Hezekiah induced them once more to live according to the law of Moses. As a divine acknowledgment of his fidelity, his reign was signalized by one of the most remarkable deliverances which Israel at any time experienced. It was the miraculous destruction by night of a vast army under Sennacherib, the king of Assyria, who had invaded the land while prosecuting a war against Egypt, and demanded the surrender of Jerusalem.

In Hezekiah's reign the public career of the prophet Isaiah came to an end. He was called to be a prophet in the year that King Uzziah died, and his earlier prophetic discourses were devoted to denouncing the wickedness of the people under the reigns of Jotham and Ahaz. These should be read in connection with what is said in Kings and Chronicles of these two kings. While the latter books give the political history, Isaiah lifts the curtain from the state of society among the people, and shows how hideous it was. He was the constant supporter and adviser of Hezekiah in all his good undertakings, and many chapters of his book, up to the thirty-ninth, are to be studied in connection with Hezekiah's reign. The last twenty-seven chapters look forward to the captivity of Judah, and the deliverance from it, while many passages in every part of the book look forward to the time of the Messiah.

Hezekiah's good reign was followed by that of Manasseh, the wickedest of all the kings that ever reigned in Jerusalem. His reign was a long one, continuing for fifty-five years. The true religion was utterly abolished, and all the forms of idolatry known among the surrounding nations were substituted. The temple of God was made the centre of these abominations. A whole generation of Jews grew up to mature years, and some to old age, without a chance to know the true God or to gain any knowledge of the Scriptures. Amon, the son and successor of Manasseh, continued in the ways of his father, adding two more years to this period of apostasy. When Josiah, the next king, came to the throne, he was only eight years old, and twelve more years were added to the period of darkness before he reached an age to vigorously attempt a reformation. By the providence of God, and perhaps through the agency of the prophet Zephaniah,[1] he was at this time brought under such influences that he undertook to restore the true worship, and to abolish idolatry. In his eighteenth year, when the reign of darkness and ignorance had endured for seventy-five years, a copy of the law of God was found in the temple and from reading it both the king and the people were enabled to realize the terrifying sinfulness of themselves and their fathers. A heroic effort was made by the king to bring the people to repentance, and to restore them to the favor of God; and he appeared to be successful; but the prophet Jeremiah, who had begun to prophesy in the thirteenth year of Josiah, and who lent all of his influence as a prophet to the support of the king, publicly denounced the reformation of the people as being

---

[1] See pages 46–47.

feigned and not from the heart. The first twenty chapters of his book should be studied in connection with the history of Josiah's reign, for they depict in most vivid colors the state of society and religion which had been and was still prevalent. He also predicted again and again the downfall of the kingdom in consequence of these sins. Josiah and Jeremiah were both young men when they began their joint labors for the salvation of the people, and no two young men ever fought a braver battle together with almost a whole nation combined against them.

Josiah was the last king of Judah who tried to avert the doom that was coming upon the nation according to the words of many prophets. His own fate was a tragic one, for he was slain in a battle against the king of Egypt, who was marching an army through his territory to make war upon Assyria with whom Josiah was in a friendly alliance. Only twenty-two years lay between his death and the beginning of the predicted captivity, and these were occupied by the reigns of three of his sons and one grandson, all four of whom rejected the counsel of God given through Jeremiah, and persisted in the wickedness which now characterized nearly all the people. During the whole of this time Jeremiah was the most conspicuous man in the nation, not as the counsellor and supporter of the kings, as in the days of Josiah, but as the mouthpiece of God, crying out constantly against the wickedness of king and subjects. All of his book, from the twenty-first chapter to the close, should be carefully studied in connection with the reigns of these four kings. Unfortunately, these chapters are not arranged in chronological order in the book, but in the preface to almost every prophetic discourse he tells us under what king, and in what year of his reign it was delivered. No character depicted in the Bible was more heroic than that of Jeremiah, and the account of none is more thrillingly interesting. He has been called the weeping prophet, because of the deep distress which he felt for the woes which were coming upon his people, his predictions of which they would not believe. He also suffered much violence at their hands. The little book called Lamentations is an expression in poetry of his sorrow over Jerusalem when it finally fell into the hands of the heathen.

9. Other Pre-Exilian Prophetic Books

Micah, Nahum, Habakkuk, Zephaniah, Obadiah, Ezekiel, Joel

In the preceding historical survey we have passed by several books which can better be considered in separate sections:

1. *Prophetical Books.* There are seven of these, and we shall name them in the order of time as nearly as that can be determined.

a. *Micah.* The ministry of this prophet ran through the reigns of Jotham, Ahaz and Hezekiah; and he was therefore a contemporary of Isaiah, who prophesied under the same kings. He called his book "The word of Jehovah that came to Micah the Morasthite, which he saw concerning Samaria and Jerusalem." He predicts the downfall of both these cities, and rebukes the people sharply for the sins which are bringing destruction upon them. He also predicts the restoration of the people, and it is he who uttered the plain prediction respecting the birthplace of our Lord, which was quoted to Herod by the scribes when the wise men appeared in Jerusalem. As he prophesied for so long a time, it almost certain that his small book contains but a very small part of his prophetic utterances.

b. *Nahum.* This writer does not tell us when he prophesied; but his book is called "The burden of Nineveh," and it is a prediction of the downfall and desolation of that ancient city. It was uttered after the Assyrians, whose capital Nineveh was, had invaded Judah for the last time (1.9–15); and this was done by Sennacherib in the reign of Hezekiah. Between this time and the fall of Nineveh, which occurred twenty years later (BC 625), Nahum prophesied; and this is as near as we can come to fixing his date. His little book opens with a magnificent tribute to the majesty and power of Jehovah, and his description of the battle scenes at the final siege of Nineveh is so vivid as to seem that of an eyewitness.

c. *Habakkuk.* This prophet, like Nahum, fails to tell us when he prophesied; but his opening sentences show that it was in a time of general lawlessness, and when the Chaldean invasion, which he predicts, would take place in the days of those to whom he spoke. This agrees with the wicked period near the close of Manasseh's reign or the early part of that of Josiah, for this was a period of lawlessness, and it was separated from the Chaldean invasion not less than twenty-five years nor more than forty. At this time the Chaldeans were still under the dominion of the Assyrians, and there was no human prospect of their coming into supreme power. The prayer of Habakkuk, which occupies the latter half of his book, is one of the grandest and most devout effusions in the whole Bible.

d. *Zephaniah.* This prophet traces his genealogy back four generations to Hezekiah; and as the only noted man of that name was king Hezekiah, it is supposed that he belonged to the royal family. He prophesied in the reign of Josiah (1.1); but in what part of his reign is not stated. If it was in the first thirteen years, he preceded Jeremiah (Jer 1.2), and that it was is almost certain when we consider the contents of his book; for he represents the people of Jerusalem and Judah at the time as engaged in various forms of idolatry (1.4–6), all of which were abolished by Josiah in the twelfth year of his reign. The first two chapters and part of the third are devoted to denunciations of Jerusalem for its iniquities, and predictions of destructive judgments to be brought upon her therefore. Adjacent nations are also included, especially those who had been enemies to the Jews. The last half of the third chapter is devoted to a prediction of the final deliverance of Israel from the impending calamities, and of the prosperity which was to follow. As this rousing prophetic appeal was sounded in the ears of the people in the early part of Josiah's reign, and came from the lips of a kinsman of the king, there can be little doubt that it greatly influenced the latter to undertake the reformation for which his reign is distinguished. The book should be read just after reading the reigns of Manasseh and Amon, and before reading that of Josiah. It gives an inside view of the state of society when Josiah, at twelve years of age, came to the throne, and it helps to account for the surprising fact that though his father and his grandfather had been given to idolatry, and to all manner of wickedness, he took the opposite course in overthrowing the idolatry which they had established, and in bringing the people back to the worship of Jehovah.

e. *Obadiah.* This very short book is entitled, "The Vision of Obadiah." Of the personal history of this prophet we have no information. The first part of the book (1.1–16) is a denunciation of Edom for the animosity which it had shown towards the Jews when Jerusalem was overthrown by the Chaldeans under Nebuchadnezzar, and a prediction of punishment for this unnatural enemy toward a kindred people. It was written then, after that event, and before the predicted punishment. A similar denunciation of Edom by Jeremiah (49.7–22) contains some of the same sentences employed by Obadiah, showing that one of these prophets copied from the other. As they wrote nearly at the same time, it can scarcely be determined which did the copying.

The rest of the book is devoted to predicting a more complete overthrow of Edom by the Jews (17–21); and this was fulfilled after the return of the latter from the Babylonian exile. Ezekiel, who was also a contemporary of Obadiah, has a similar prediction (25.12–14).

There is nothing said of this hostility of Edom in any of the historical books; but it crops out only in the writings of these three prophets, but also in the 137th Psalm, written in the captivity, or soon after its close, in which the author says:

"Remember, O Lord, against the children of Edom
The days of Jerusalem;
Who said, Rase it, rase it,
Even to the foundation thereof."

f. *Ezekiel.* This prophet, like Jeremiah, was a priest (1.3). He was called to be a prophet in the fifth year of king Jehoiachin's captivity, which corresponds with the fifth year of the reign of Zedekiah, the last king of Jerusalem. He was at the time among the captives in the land of the Chaldeans (1.3), and he was doubtless one of those who were carried away with Jehoiachin by Nebuchadnezzar. When he began to prophesy, Jeremiah had already been engaged in the work about thirty years; and as Ezekiel was now thirty years old (1.1), he had been brought up from infancy under the teaching of Jeremiah. He continued to prophesy until the 27th year of Jehoiachin's captivity (29.17), and perhaps longer. His first six or seven years lapped over the last six or seven of Jeremiah, and during that period they were fellow workers, the one in Jerusalem and the other in the vicinity of Babylon, both foretelling the speedy downfall of the kingdom of Judah, and exhorting the people to repentance. The first half of Ezekiel's book, or twenty-four of its forty-eight chapters, is devoted to these topics. He employs a great many very strange symbols, both in word and action, some of which are very difficult of interpretation; but he also teaches with great plainness of speech many lessons of extreme importance, not for his own age only, but for all generations of men. The reader will readily distinguish the chapters containing these lessons, and he should study them until they become very familiar.

The latter half of the book contains predictions respecting the restoration of Israel and Judah, and their subsequent career in their own country. In this part there are descriptions and symbols still more mysterious than those in the first part, some of which have never been satisfactorily interpreted. Like the other prophets, he gives very little information about his personal history, and nothing is now known respecting the time or place of his death. Had he lived to be one hundred years old, he would have seen the end of the captivity; but as that is improbable, he most probably died in Babylon.

g. *Joel.* Nothing is known of the personal history of Joel except that he was the son of Pethuel (1.1). He does not say, like the majority of the prophets, in what reign or reigns he prophesied, and the indications of date in his book are so indefinite that commentators have differed very greatly as to the time in which he wrote, some placing him among the earliest, and some among the latest of the prophets. Fortunately, the value of the book to us does not depend upon its exact date.

The first part of the book (1.1–11, 17) contains a prediction of a visitation of locusts such as had not been known to previous generations in the land of Israel (1.2–3). The description is wonderfully vivid, made so in part by speaking frequently as if the scene were passing before the eyes of the prophet. The language employed in parts of the description is such that some interpreters have understood the whole as a symbolic representation of desolating armies of men.

Next after this visitation the prophet foretells a prosperous condition of the country (2.18–27), and then he predicts the outpouring of the Holy Spirit. The apostle Peter on the day of Pentecost quoted the prediction as being then in part fulfilled (2.28–32; Comp. Acts 2.16–21). This is the most notable feature of Joel's prophesying. It was given to him among the prophets to make the most distinct prediction of the great event which inaugurated the kingdom of God on earth.

The rest of the prophecy is taken up with a prediction of God's judgments on the nations surrounding Judah for the cruelties which they had visited on his people. It makes no mention of the kingdom of Israel; and this circumstance, together with the fact that all its local allusions have reference to Judah, shows that the prophet lived in the southern kingdom. There is no particular part of the history with which the book has any special connection, or on which it throws light.

10. The Poetical Books[1]

Job, The Psalms, Proverbs, Ecclesiastes, The Song of Songs

We have passed by this class of books, not because they are of later date than those mentioned in the last two sections, but because they could not be considered earlier without a break in the thread of the history.

1. *Job*. This is a poetical book with an introduction, or prologue, and a sequel or epilogue, in prose. The former gives the character and circumstances of the man, together with a vain attempt of Satan to prove that his motive in serving God was a selfish one. After the failure of Satan's attempt, which left Job in a state of destitution and extreme suffering, three of his friends come to console him, and after a time of mournful silence, they enter into a debate with him as to the cause of his affliction. They unitedly assume that his sufferings were due to some secret sin of which he had been guilty, and they base their conclusion on the general proposition that God never afflicts the righteous. Job denies their proposition, and defends himself the best he can, until they have had three rounds of speeches, the friends speaking in regular rotation and Job answering each one separately. Then a younger man, named Elihu, whose presence had not been men-

---

[1] It is somewhat difficult to classify accurately the books of this section. "Poetical" does not fully describe them, since Ecclesiastes is not poetry, and then other parts of the Old Testament material are poetic, especially Isaiah 40–66. Perhaps a division of these books may be made into "Wisdom Books," including Job, Proverbs, Ecclesiastes and the Song of Songs, and "Devotional," in which latter class the Psalms would be placed. —W.

tioned, makes a speech, and finally God himself speaks from a whirlwind. In the sequel God decides that Job was right on the question debated; commands the three friends to bring an offering to the altar that Job might intercede for them, and restores Job to double the earthly prosperity which he enjoyed before the trial began. The speeches are not limited in subject matter to the question in debate; but all of them take a wide range of thought, and they contain some of the most sublime and edifying poetry to be found in any literature.

The question has been raised very often whether Job was a real or imaginary person; but it seems to be settled by the prophet Ezekiel and the apostle James, each of whom makes statements which imply the reality of his existence, his high character, his sufferings and his deliverance (Ezek 14.12–20; Jas 5.10–11). But while Job, and also his four friends, were real persons, their speeches were not delivered in the poetical form in which we have them, for this would be impossible without miraculous aid; and that they did not enjoy this appears from the fact that all of them said things for which they were censured. Doubtless the author of the book, who is unknown to us, with the argument for a starting point, worked the speeches into the form in which we have them.

The times at which Job lived cannot be definitely determined, but it was before the time of Ezekiel who refers to him as an example of eminent righteousness.

2. *The Psalms.* A glance through this book in the Revised Version will show that it consists of five books in one, each ending with a doxology and an Amen. These five collections were made at different times, and by different compilers; for the Psalms were not all written at one time or in the lifetime of one man. One of them (90) is ascribed to Moses, and some of them (*e.g.,* 137) were as late as the Babylonian exile.[2] Their dates and authorship are ascertained, so far as these can now be known, partly by the inscrip-

---

[2]Some students of the Psalms find in certain of them evidence of a date later than the return from Babylon, and in three or four (44; 77; 79; 83) indications of origin in the Maccabean period. —W.

tions printed above some of them, and partly by a comparison of their personal and historical allusions with the history of the people of Israel. The superscriptions are not a part of the text, but they are of very ancient date; and while they are not infallible, they are in the main, at least, reliable. By these, seventy-three Psalms are ascribed to David,[3] and this has led to styling the collection as a whole the Psalms of David, the title being taken from the principal author. This title, however, is not a part of the sacred text. The title in the original text was the Hebrew word for Praises; and the Greek translators originated the title now in use.

In order to read the Psalms with the greatest profit, every one which contains personal or historical allusions should be read in connection with the events alluded to. A good reference Bible will usually point these out to the reader; but it is better still to have such a knowledge of the historical books, that the events alluded to will be readily recalled by the allusions.

The sentiments expressed in the Psalms came from the hearts of the authors, and they show the best effects of the law of Moses, and the experience of Israel on the souls of devout men under that dispensation. They were written under so great a variety of circumstances that they express the sentiment of godly men in almost any condition in which men find themselves to-day; and therefore they are adapted to our edification in all the varied scenes of life. One who is familiar with them can readily turn to such as will comfort him in any sorrow, cheer him in any despondency, and furnish expression to his deepest gratitude and most fervid thanksgiving. They are marked, however, by one defect as compared with the sentiments inculcated by Christ, and that is their occasional expression of hatred toward enemies. Under that dispensation war was tolerated, and this rendered it impossible to suppress hostile feelings towards the enemy; consequently the best of men felt at

---

[3]It is usually agreed among scholars that whatever may have been the number of Psalms written by David, the following are certainly his in the order of the chief periods of his life: Psalms referring to his early life, either written then, or recollections of the period written later, 19; 8; 29; 23 ; his persecution by Saul, 11; 7 the ark brought to Zion, 24; 101; 15; David's wars, 18; 21; 110; 9; David's sin and repentance, 51; 32; Absalom's rebellion, 3; 4; 21; 63; 12. —W.

liberty to indulge and express these sentiments. In reading the Psalms we should carefully abstain from entering into such sentiments with the authors, and should pass them by as imperfections of a preparatory dispensation of the divine government.

3. *Proverbs.* A proverb strictly speaking, is a sentence which expresses briefly and strongly some practical truth. In this sense this book is not wholly made up of proverbs; for the first nine chapters contain a series of short poems of a different character, yet they are all full of practical lessons such as proverbs teach; and consequently, they are not out of place in a book bearing the general title of Proverbs.

The second division of the book, beginning with chapter ten, has the heading "The Proverbs of Solomon," and here the proverbs properly speaking, begin. They extend to 22.16, and constitute the largest division of the book, giving the name to the whole. These chapters contain 375 separate proverbs, only a small number in comparison with the 3,000 which Solomon is said to have composed (1 Kgs 4.32). These proverbs are full of practical wisdom.

From chapter 22.17 to the close of chapter 24, the matter and form are much the same as in the first part of the book. Then follow five chapters with the titles, "These also are Proverbs of Solomon, which the men of Hezekiah king of Judah copied out." Thus the book was in part a growth.

The last section of the book, chapter 31, is entitled, "The Words of King Lemuel; the oracle which his mother taught him." Who Lemuel was is not known. His words and the whole book, close with a description of "A Virtuous Woman," which presents an ideal of womanhood.[4]

---

[4]It will be seen that the book is made up of several sections, of which the oldest seem to be 10.1–20.16 and chapters 25–29. These are called collections of Solomon's Proverbs. In addition there are the "Sayings of the Wise," 22.17–24, "The Words of Agur," chapter 30, "The Words of King Lemuel," 31.1–9, the acrostic poem in praise of the Ideal Woman, 31.10–31, and chapters 1–9, which were perhaps written by the compiler of the whole collection, who named the entire work the Proverbs of Solomon, thus using the wise King as the common denominator of all the material of which he was known to have set the pattern for later days. The relation of Solomon to the Proverb literature is the same as that of David to the Psalter. Each set in motion a type of literary activity to which others added through centuries. —W.

4. *Ecclesiastes.* The printed title of this book is "Ecclesiastes or the Preacher;" but the title which it gives to itself is, "The Words of the Preacher, the son of David, king in Jerusalem" (1.1). The Hebrew word rendered preacher, is *Koheleth.* This was rendered by the authors of the Septuagint, *Ecclesiastes;* and this, anglicized, gives us the word commonly used as the title of the book. Many scholars now use the Hebrew word when speaking of the book, and call it Koheleth. The preacher meant is undoubtedly Solomon; for he is the only son or descendant of David who reigned in Jerusalem, and whose experiences correspond to those mentioned in the text. There are some who doubt whether Solomon wrote the book, and some who are very positive that he did not; yet even these admit that whoever the writer was, he attempted to set forth the sentiment of Solomon, and wrote in his person.

We might look upon the whole book as a sermon (and it would not be a very long one) in which the preacher sets forth the vanity, or emptiness of this life considered within itself. His text, to use a modern expression, is "Vanity of Vanities, all is Vanity" (1.2); and if this life ends all, we must admit the truth of the proposition. There are some passages in the book which are quite obscure, and some which have the appearance of being contradictory to others; but when we keep in view the author's purpose of looking at this life as if it were our only state of existence these difficulties nearly all disappear. In the final conclusion the author says: "This is the end of all matter: All hath been heard; fear God, and keep his commandments; for this is the whole duty of man; for God shall bring every work into judgment, and every hidden thing, whether it be good or whether it be evil."

This book should be read in connection with the life of Solomon, which is set forth in the books of First Kings and Second Chronicles. With this piece of history fresh in the memory, the beauty of the sermon will be more highly appreciated, and its power more seriously felt.[5]

---

[5]There are many considerations that make the Solomonic authorship of Ecclesiastes extremely improbable, and indicate that a writer in one of the latest periods of Old Testament history

5. *The Song of Songs.* The title which this short poem assigns itself is, "The Song of Songs, which is Solomon's" (1.1). If there is any book in the Bible which found a place in it by a mistake or misjudgment of those who put the inspired book together, it must be this; for it is so totally unlike all the rest that it is difficult to see what connection it can have with the general design of the whole. Many interpreters have affected to find in it a parabolic meaning, and even a foreshadowing of the love of the Church of Christ; while others have regarded it as nothing more than a love-song with a very obscure connection of thought. According to either view it has afforded little edification to the great majority of Bible readers; and unless some significance can be found in it hereafter which has not yet been pointed out, it will continue to be but little read, and of but little practical value.[6]

---

used Solomon as a character into whose mouth he could put the words which he desired to speak. He was troubled by the fact that nothing that one possesses or does seems to give satisfaction. He did not even consider a future life probable, for the hope of eternal life was only revealed in its fulness by Christ. The answer which Ecclesiastes makes to the problem of life is that one should receive all its good with thankfulness, and use wisely all that God gives. —W.

[6]It is a dramatic poem. The earlier interpretation made it an epithalamium, or marriage song, recording the love and marriage of Solomon and his queen. The later, and now generally accepted interpretation makes the heroine a maiden of Shulem or Shunem, whom King Solomon takes into his court and attempts by flattery and magnificent promises to separate her from her lover, to whom, however, she remains faithful and is at last restored. The book is a beautiful tribute to true and constant love, which no wealth can dazzle and no power can overawe. It is also a refreshing picture of the virtues to be found among the common people in an age of the greatest splendor and of growing corruption in the court of Solomon. The spiritual lessons of the book are not to be found in mystical allusions to Christ and the Church, but in the purity and constancy of love, lessons needed in no age more than our own. —W.

11. The Books of Exile[1]

Daniel, Esther

We have now made mention of all the books of the Old Testament connected with events preceding the Babylonian exile. We come next to the two books concerned exclusively with events which occurred in the exile, the books of Daniel and Esther.

1. *Daniel*. This book, as also the experiences of Daniel himself spans the whole period of the captivity of Judah; for it begins in the third year of Jehoiakim, king of Judah, eight years before the captivity of Jehoiachin (1.1), and it ends in the third year of Cyrus, king of Persia, two years after the captivity of Judah ended (10.1; Ezra 1.1–3). It indirectly represents itself as having been written by Daniel; for although he is spoken of in the first six chapters in the third person, as was common in historical narration, he speaks in the first person in the other six. He was connected with the royal family of Judah (1.3), and it is probable that he and his companions were taken to Babylon by Nebuchadnezzar as hostages for the good conduct of Jehoiakim who was tributary to the Babylonians. He saw the beginning and the end of the Babylonian Empire, and he was more or less connected with the palace through the whole period.

The events recorded in the first six chapters were evidently intended by the Lord for two distinct purposes: first, to keep the captive Jews from losing their faith in Jehovah; and second, to

---

[1]In addition to the books here named as belonging to the Exile Period, it will be remembered that portions of Jeremiah and Ezekiel came from the years of the captivity, and the whole of Isaiah, 40–66, deals with this situation. —W.

make the power and majesty of Jehovah known to the heathen population of the Babylonian Empire. The Jews must have been strongly tempted, when they saw the Holy City and God's holy temple in ruins, and themselves transported into a foreign land by a heathen nation, to think either that Jehovah had abandoned them in violation of many promises made to their fathers, or that he was not able to cope with the gods of the great heathen empire. Either conclusion would cause them to fall in with the religion of their conquerors, and thus to forfeit all the good things which Jehovah had promised them. On the other hand, the conquerors, ascribing as they and all the heathen nations did, their victories to the superior power of the gods they worshipped, unavoidably reached the conclusion that their gods were far more powerful than Jehovah. But this false reasoning was corrected by the series of occurrences which are here recorded.

The other six chapters of Daniel, all prophetic, made many clear revelations of the destiny provided for Israel; and, although some of them were obscure then, and are more or less so to this day, others were almost as intelligible as history, and proved a great source of comfort and encouragement to the Jews in the fierce conflicts through which they passed between the exile and the coming of Christ.

2. *Esther.* The events recorded in this book took place in the reign of Ahasuerus, otherwise called Xerxes. His Persian name, spelled in English letters, reads thus: Khshayarsha. The Greeks, in trying to render it into their language, got it Xerxes; and the Hebrews, Ahasuerus. The latter comes nearer the original, but European nations have adopted in common usage the Greek rendering. This king began to reign about fifty years after the decree of Cyrus permitting the Jews to return to their own land, and consequently, the events of the book, though they belong to the history of the Jews in exile, occurred between fifty and sixty years after the close of the seventy years predicted by Jeremiah. In other words, they occurred among those Jews who chose, after the proclamation of Cyrus, to remain in foreign lands.

The book gives an account of a crisis in the history of the Jewish people. A decree was sent forth by the king that every Jew in his kingdom should be put to death on a certain day. The circumstance which led to the issuing of this decree, and the measures by which the calamity was averted, constitute the subject matter of the book, and they present a most remarkable series of divine providences. In Esther the name of God is not once mentioned. The reader is left to discover God's hand for himself.

12. The Post-Exilic Books

Ezra, Nehemiah, Haggai, Zechariah, Malachi, Intertestamental Period

The books written in Jerusalem after the return from the exile, now commonly called post-exilic, are five in number, *viz*. Ezra, Nehemiah, Haggai, Zechariah, and Malachi. We shall speak of them in this order.

1. *Ezra.* This book begins, as Chronicles left off, with the decree of Cyrus for the release of the captives and their return to their native land.[1] It gives a little fuller account of this decree, and also an account of the return of of the first caravan of Jews under the command of Zerubbabel, called also "Sheshbazzar the prince of Judah" (1.8; 2.2; 3.8). He was the prince of Judah, in the sense that being a grandson of Jehoiachin, the last king, he would have been entitled to the throne if Israel had been an independent nation (1 Chron 3.17–19). The reader will be surprised to find, from this account, how small a number of the Jews saw fit to take advantage of the offer made to them by Cyrus. The rest had become satisfied to remain in foreign lands, where they were doubtless prosperous in the main, rather than return to a depopulated country, and go through the hardship of rebuilding their cities and homes. This reflects the more credit on the zeal and faith of those who did enter into this hard undertaking. The joy with which they made the journey had

---

[1]By comparing Ezra 1.1–3 with 2 Chronicles. 36.22–23 it will be seen that the two books were evidently one originally, but were separated, perhaps by accident, in the middle of verse 3, and the earlier verses were copied from the 2 Chronicles passage to make the beginning of what became a new book.

been depicted in the most glowing and hyperbolical imagery. Read in this connection chapters 40–52 of the book of Isaiah, and see in what rapturous strains the writer dwells upon this theme, returning to it again and again amid other topics of which he writes.

All went well with the people in their efforts to rebuild the temple during the rest of the reign of Cyrus; but in subsequent reigns the Samaritans, as the mixed races were then called that inhabited the territory of the northern tribes, obtained a royal decree for the suspension of the work, and it was not till the second year of the reign of Darius that the work was renewed. Then the two prophets Haggai and Zechariah encouraged the people to renew the work, and they did so without waiting to hear from the king. Another effort was made to stop them, but when the king was heard from it was with a decree that the work should not be hindered. The account of these proceedings in chapters 1–6, is full of interest and instruction. The time from the return till the completion of the temple was twenty-one years, as is known from the intervening reigns of Persian kings.

Between the sixth and seventh chapters of Ezra there is a gap of time of fifty-seven years, extending from the sixth year of Darius to the seventh year of Artaxerxes (6.15; 7.8). In this interval Xerxes had reigned, and made his famous expedition into Greece, and the events of the book of Esther had taken place. Why Ezra leaves it blank is not known, but perhaps, on account of the troublous character of the times he had nothing special to record that was not already written in Esther. This book marks the division between the very distinct parts of the book of Ezra, the first six chapters giving the history of the caravan which returned under Zerubbabel until they had completed the temple, while the second part gives the personal labors of Ezra. He came to Jerusalem with a letter from the king and authorizing him to establish the law of God as the law of the land, and to enforce it if need be, by all the usual penalties of violated law (7.25–26). This was a matter of supreme importance to the Jews; for hitherto they had been governed in civil matters only by the laws of Persia. Ezra, being a priest and a scribe, had by hard study specially qualified himself for this important task, and he proved himself eminently worthy of the confidence which the king reposed in him. He preserves a list of those who reformed under his entreaties, so that their sons and daughters after them might know that their fathers were among the true hearted who turned back to the Lord when rebuked for their sins.

2. *Nehemiah.* In the ancient Hebrew manuscripts the books of Ezra and Nehemiah were written as if they were one; but the title, "The Words of Nehemiah, the son of Hachaliah" (1.1) clearly indicate the beginning of another book, and justify the separation which was made in the Greek translation at an early period. While the temple was rebuilt by Zerubbabel, it was the work of Nehemiah to rebuild the city walls. He went from Babylon for this purpose, thirteen years after Ezra went there to establish the law. That which moved him to the undertaking is set forth in the first chapter. The distress there depicted, which overwhelmed him on hearing that "the city, the place of his father's sepulchres," was lying waste and its gates burned with fire, is accounting for if he had previously thought that since the return of so many captives the walls had been rebuilt; though it is supposed by some scholars that they had been rebuilt and had been again thrown down within the thirteen years just mentioned.

It will be seen by reading these six chapters, that Nehemiah was equally zealous and self-sacrificing with Ezra, but quite different in his way. While the latter was a priest by descent, and a scribe by profession, Nehemiah held a civil office, being cup-bearer to the king; and he had no scruple, therefore, about asking the king for a military escort when he obtained permission to go to Jerusalem (2.9). He acted as governor of the land for twelve years, yet he received no salary; he made no purchase of lands, though doubtless there was a tempting opportunity for speculation in them; he made his own servants work on the wall; and he fed at his table a daily average of one hundred and fifty men, Jews and visitors from other lands (5.14–17). His expenditure must have amounted to a very considerable fortune.

The other seven chapters of the book are occupied with some details of Nehemiah's government of the people after the completion of the walls.

At the end of his leave of absence from the king he came back to Babylon, and "after certain days" he came again to Jerusalem (2.6; 13.6–7). During his absence intermarriages with the heathen had again sprung up, and other abuses crept in.

The narrative closes without a hint as to the subsequent life or death of either Nehemiah or Ezra; and thus ends the history contained in the Old Testament.

3. *Haggai.* In this little book we are taken back in time to the second year of Darius, and the first day of the sixth month of that year (1.1). There had been a failure of crops in the land, and the prophet came to Zerubbabel and Joshua the priest with "the word of the Lord," telling them that it was because the people had been building good houses for themselves, and neglecting to build the Lord's house. The result was, that these men and the people were aroused, and began the work anew on the twenty-fourth day of the same month. This was before the issuing of the decree of Darius, giving them permission to renew the building (6.1–5). Having the Lord's permission and command, they went to work without waiting for that of the king. This much is set forth in the first chapter.

About a month later, as we read in the second chapter, the word of the Lord came again to the prophet, promising that, although this house that they were building seemed to the old people as nothing when compared with Solomon's, it should at a future day be filled with glory, and the latter glory of it should be greater than the former; "and in this place I will give peace, saith Jehovah of Hosts." This prediction had evident reference to the connection of Jesus and his apostles with that house; for by this its greatest glory was attained.

About two months later, on the 24th of the ninth month of the same year, two other messages were brought by Haggai, the first reminding the people again that the crop failure was a punishment sent by the Lord, but promising that from that day forth he would bless them. The second was a personal message to Zerubbabel, promising him that while Jehovah was going to overthrow all the nations and kingdoms, he would take him and make him "a signet." As Zerubbabel was a lineal ancestor of our Lord Jesus Christ, this seems to be an allusion to the high honor conferred on him in making him such.

From this we see that the five brief messages which were sent by God through this prophet, were all delivered within the space of three months, and were all intended to encourage the people in the arduous labor of rebuilding the temple.

4. *Zechariah*. While Haggai began his prophesying in the sixth month of the second year of Darius, and closed it in the ninth month, Zechariah began in the eighth month of the same year. His first message was a very brief one, exhorting the people not be as the fathers had been, to whom the former prophets had spoken, but to take warning from the fate that befell them. Here is found that well known and beautiful passage, "Your fathers, where are they? and the prophets, do they live forever?" (1.1–6).

About three months later, on the 24th day of the eleventh month, in the same year of Darius, he brought his second message, consisting of eight symbolical and very curious visions, all of which, interpreted to him by an angel, gave encouragement to the people with respect to the temple (1.1–6, 15). Thus we see that the first work of Zechariah, like all the work of Haggai, was to co-operate with each other and with Zerubbabel and Joshua the priest, in pushing forward the reconstruction of the temple. This was necessary to the fulfillment of God's purposes and promises respecting Israel and the coming kingdom of Christ.

From the beginning of the seventh chapter to the close of the book the prophet is occupied with other themes, and his style rises at times to the grandeur which characterizes the finest passages in Isaiah.[2] He rebukes all manner of sins, and calls powerfully to

---

[2]The unity of the book of Zechariah is one of the open questions of Biblical study. Indications of a different horizon and authorship are found by some scholars in the sections 9–1 and 12–14. —W.

righteous living. He predicts the gathering of the ten tribes, and the downfall of those nations which oppressed Israel. He foresees calamities yet to befall Jerusalem, more disastrous than those of her recent experiences; but these are to be followed by a time of peace and holiness. In the midst of these predictions we find several passages which are quoted in the New Testament as being fulfilled in connection with the life of Jesus (1.12–13; 13.1–7).

5. *Malachi.* As Nehemiah was the last of the Old Testament historians, Malachi was the last of the prophets; and they co-operated with each other; for while Malachi, unlike Haggai and Zechariah, does not give the date of his message, the contents of it show clearly that he spoke after the temple had been completed and the regular service therein had been renewed. As he makes no allusion to the troubles about rebuilding the walls, this work also seems to have been completed. And as he rebukes the people for intermarriage with the heathen, this agrees with the state of things when Nehemiah came the second time to Jerusalem, and broke up that practice.

The book has the form of a single discourse by the prophet. He begins with the fact that God had loved Jacob and hated Esau, where the two brothers are put for the nations that sprang from them; and he predicts disaster yet to befall the latter (1.1–5).

He then rebukes the priests for treating with contempt the law of sacrifices, a corruption which grew out of their avarice (1.6–11, 14). He next predicts the coming of the Messiah to the temple, and the work of purification and separation which he will execute (2.17–3.6). Turning back to his own time he rebukes the people severely for withholding their tithes and offerings, and for pretending that there was no profit in serving the Lord (3.7–15). He predicts the final blessedness of those that feared the Lord, and the destruction of those who feared him not (3.16–4.3).

As a most fitting close of the Old Testament, he looks back and says to the people, "Remember ye the law of Moses my servant, which I commanded unto him in Horeb for all Israel, even statutes and judgments;" and then he looks forward to the work of John the Baptist, and says, "Behold, I will send you Elijah the prophet before the great and terrible day of the Lord come. And he shall turn the heart of the fathers to the children, and the heart of the children to their fathers; lest I come and smite the earth with a curse."

───────────

We have now given a brief introduction to every one of the thirty-nine books of the Old Testament, and we have come down to within about four and a half centuries of the birth of Christ, with which the New Testament begins. Of that interval we have no inspired history, and of much of it we have no history at all. The most than can now be known of it is derived from the books called The Apocrypha, some of which are edifying, some historical, and some fabulous. It would be well for the student to read them after becoming reasonably familiar with the Old Testament. Josephus gives a history of this period as he derived it from these sources. Some portions of it are thrillingly interesting, and a knowledge of it enables one to better understand the views and practices of the Jews in the days of Christ and the apostles.[3]

───────────

[3]See list of apocryphal books in the Appendix. —W.

13. Divisions of the New Testament

The general divisions of the New Testament are well known. The four Gospels are biographical; Acts of the Apostles is historical; the Epistles, as their name indications, are epistolary, and the Revelation, or the Apocalypse as scholars generally prefer to style it, is descriptive and prophetic.

The Gospels do not pretend to give a complete biography of Christ; but only a few such facts in his career as serve to establish his claim to be the Christ the Son of God; and a few specimens of his teaching and his predictions. One of them declares the first to be its purpose (John 20.31), and the contents of the others show that the same is true of them. John also shows the fragmentary character of his narrative by saying, in hyperbolical terms, that if all that Jesus did should be written, he supposes that the world itself could not contain the books that would be written (21.25).

The book of Acts is a general history of the church for about thirty years from its beginning; the Epistles are communications from certain of the Apostles, that is, from Paul, James, Peter, Jude, and John, all addressed to churches or to individual Christians; and the Apocalypse sets forth in the main the destiny of the church.

14. The Gospels and Acts

Matthew, Mark, Luke, John, Acts

These are not the first books of the New Testament that were written; for, as we shall see later, some of Paul's epistles preceded them; but they are first in the order of the events of which they speak, and for this reason they very properly occupy the first part of the book when all are printed in one volume. Having stated in the preceding section their general design, we shall now consider them separately.

1. *Matthew.* This writer introduces Jesus, in the first verse of the book, as "The son of David, the son of Abraham." By this title he designates him as the promised seed of David who was to sit upon David's throne and reign forever, and he also keeps in mind the ancient promise to Abraham of a seed in whom all the nations of the earth were to be blessed. In other words, this introduces him as the Messiah, or the Christ; and it shows that Matthew's main purpose was to set forth the Messiahship of Jesus, rather than his divinity. With this agree the contents of the book; for while the Sonship of Jesus is by no means overlooked in the narrative, but is clearly and emphatically set forth, his Messiahship is the logical point chiefly aimed at; hence the many quotations from the Old Testament of predictions and types which were fulfilled in his person and in his work. Matthew has more of these than have all three of the other Gospels. In harmony with the same purpose Matthew devotes more of his space than any of the others to the teachings of Jesus, considerably more than half his book being made up of his formal speeches, besides many remarks made

in the course of conversations with friends and foes. To such an extent is this true, that a Christian writer of the second century called his book "The Oracles," meaning thereby, divine utterances. This was an attempt to give a name to the book derived from the chief part of its contents. In consequence of this peculiarity of the book, as well as its location at the beginning of the volume, Matthew is more read by the people, and more familiar to them, than any of the other Gospels, or any other book, perhaps, in the Bible.

The book naturally divided itself into three distinct parts: the first (1.1–4.12) giving the genealogy of Jesus; his birth; some of the events of his infancy; his baptism and his temptation; the second, his ministry in Galilee (4.13–19.1); and the third, the events from his departure out of Galilee till his resurrection from the dead (19.1–28.20). The last division, though it occupies only six months of the three years and more of his ministry, fills nearly as much space as the account of the whole period preceding this, showing the importance attached by the author to the scenes connected with the last sufferings, the death, and the resurrection of the Lord.[1]

2. *Mark.* This writer was not an apostle, but he was the son of a certain woman in Jerusalem whose name was Mary, and whose house was a place of resort for the disciples (Acts 12.12). She was an aunt of Barnabas, seeing that Mark was his cousin (Col 4.10). Having grown up in Jerusalem, where his mother was prominent among the disciples, he must himself have been acquainted with the apostles, and probably with Jesus. It is said by early Christian writers that in writing his Gospel he gave the account of Jesus which Peter was in the habit of giving in his discourses; and there is much in his narrative to confirm this tradition, especially the fact that he tells plainly everything that Peter did or said which was not creditable to him, and omits nearly all that was. This is the way that Peter would do if he was as modest as we suppose him to have been.

---

[1] The Gospel of Matthew was addressed primarily to the Jewish people, and therefore uses the Old Testament material bearing upon the life of Christ. It is the national Gospel, and its themes are Jesus the Messiah, the Teacher and the Rejected King. —W.

Mark introduces Jesus at once as the Son of God, saying in the first line of his book, "The beginning of the gospel of Jesus Christ, the Son of God." This shows that his main purpose, logically, was to prove the divinity rather than the Messiahship of Jesus. In this he differs from Matthew; and in carrying out this plan he devotes a much larger per cent. of his space to miracles than does any other of the four, seeing that it is this, rather than prophecies fulfilled, that proves his divinity. He makes a different "beginning" from that of Matthew, in that he begins with the preaching of John the Baptist, and Matthew begins with the genealogy and birth of Jesus.

No one who is familiar with Matthew can read Mark without noticing a striking similarity between them in the facts that they relate, and sometimes in the words that they employ; but on close comparison of the two it will be seen that in almost, if not quite all these instances, Mark has some additional items which distinguish his account from Matthew's. The student should constantly keep his eye open for these; for they not only show the difference between the two writers, making each stand out before the mind by himself, but they are necessary to a full knowledge of the incidents with which they are connected. The same may be said in reference to events mentioned by three, or by all of the Gospel writers. Study all, and combine the particulars given by all.

Mark's book is divided into two parts, in the first of which he confines himself to the ministry in Galilee, as Matthew does in his second part; and in the second, after reporting a few conversations beyond the Jordan, he confines himself to the closing scenes in Jerusalem. To this second part, although the time included in it is only six months, he devotes seven out of his sixteen chapters, thus showing as Matthew does, that he regarded this as the part of the life of Jesus that was most important for his readers to be acquainted with.[2] Luke and John follow the same plan.

---

[2] Mark's Gospel has been called the Gospel of Power. Jesus is the worker of miracles, the incarnation of power. As such the book would commend itself to the Roman type of mind, in which power held the chief place. —W.

3. *Luke.* The third Gospel differs from the first and second more than the latter do from each other. It records some events in common with the other two, but the plan of the author, as well as his subject matter, is quite different. In comparing his accounts with those of the other two, the differences sometimes appear much like contradictions, and so they have been pronounced by unfriendly writers. But it is never just to charge two or more writers with contradicting one another, which is the same as charging one or more of them with error, when there is any reasonable supposition that will permit all their statements to be true. Sometimes we have to study very carefully before we can find such a supposition, but as we are bound in justice to do it when we can, we must be slow to charge contradictions. This is a right rule in respect to all writers and speakers, and more especially should we observe it in respect to the inspired writers of the New Testament.

Luke's first part, like Matthew's, is devoted to the infancy and the early life of Jesus, concluding with his temptation; and the amount of space which he gives to it about the same as Matthew's, but he fills it with incidents nearly all of which are different from those given by Matthew. In order to learn all we can about this part of our Lord's life, we have to study the first part of Luke and that of Matthew together; and it would be well for the student to do this before he reads farther in this Gospel.

In the second part, Luke gives his attention, like Matthew and Mark, to the ministry of Jesus in Galilee, saying nothing about some visits to Jerusalem which we know from John's Gospel were made during this period. This part extends from 4.14 to 9.62, less space than is given it by either Matthew or Mark. Then follows the part of Luke in which he gives the most new information, and the whole of it is both instructive and charming. It includes chapters ten to eighteen, more than either of the other parts. His last, or fourth part, like that of the other two Gospels, is devoted to the closing scenes of the last six months, and it includes his last six chapters.

Luke was a physician, as we learn from Paul (Col 4.14); and as Paul in the same passage seems to distinguish him from "those of the circumcision" (10, 14), it is inferred that he was a Gentile. If so he was the only Gentile who wrote any part of the New Testament. Like Mark, he was not an apostle; and consequently he did not write as an eye-witness; but he informs us, in the opening paragraph of his book, that he had obtained his information from eye-witnesses and ministers of the word, and that he had traced everything accurately from the beginning. As his book is addressed to one Theophilus, whose name is a Greek word, it appears that he intended it primarily for Greek readers. He addresses Theophilus by the title "most excellent," the usual Greek form of address to a man of high rank in the political world, from which it appears that at least a few such men had been brought into the church when Luke's Gospel was written.[3]

All three of the Gospels which we have now noticed are supposed, to have been written not earlier than the year 60 AD.

4. *John.* This fourth Gospel differs very greatly in its subject matter from the other three. The latter are so much alike, that they are styled by scholars, "Synoptic," that is, taking the same view. But John carefully avoided repeating what the others had written, so that he has very few events in common with them; and when he had he gives details which they had omitted. This difference is accounted for by the fact, that writing much later, he had seen what they wrote, and cared not to repeat it; while their similarity to one another is accounted for by their having written without seeing one another's productions. They doubtless wrote those incidents in the life of the Savior which had been commonly related by the apostles in their preaching.

John's is the only Gospel which is chronological throughout. By counting the feasts of the Jews which Christ attended, all of which are mentioned in this Gospel, we ascertain that there were three years from the visit to Jerusalem mentioned in the second chapter, to the one at which he was crucified. If we could only

---

[3]Luke's Gospel is his introduction to the story of the Apostolic Church and the ministry of Paul which is given in Acts. It emphasizes the compassionate love of Jesus for humanity. It is the Gospel of Society. —W.

ascertain how long it was from his baptism till that first visit, we would know the exact duration of his ministry; but at this point the chronology is not given.

John begins with a very profound statement of the eternal and divine existence of Jesus before his advent into the world; and in harmony with this beginning he makes the divinity of the Lord throughout his book much more prominent than his Messiah-ship. In this he is like Mark; but unlike Mark he mentions comparatively few of the miracles; and he depends for his argument mainly on what Jesus said about himself. Consequently, we find Jesus in this Gospel saying much more about himself as the Son of God than in any or all of the others.

One very remarkable fact about John's Gospel is that all of the events which he records occurred on only about thirty days, although the time between the first and the last was more than three years. In Mark we find the incidents of only seven or eight days more, if we leave out the forty of the Temptation, and in Luke and Matthew, less than a hundred. Any one of the four, if printed separately, would make only a small tract. This is a very striking proof that these men were under the controlling power of the Holy Spirit; for we may safely say that no four men ever lived, who, with such a life to write about, would have written so little if they had been left to themselves.[4]

5. *Acts of Apostles.* This book most properly follows the four Gospels in our printed New Testament, not because it was written later; for it was written about the same time with the first three Gospels, and much earlier than the fourth; but because the facts recorded in it occurred next, and because this is its place from a logical point of view. It was after the resurrection of Jesus with an account of which each of the Gospels closes, that Jesus gave to the apostles their commission to go and preach, having forbidden them to do so while he was yet in the flesh. This book

---

[4]John's Gospel is the universal Gospel, the Gospel of the Incarnation, the Gospel of Spiritual Insight. It is the Gospel of the heart of Christ as contrasted with the more objective writing of the Synoptists. —W.

gives an account of their going in obedience to this command, and preaching to the world. Moreover, it shows how men under apostolic preaching, were brought to Christ and became members of his church; and as the Gospels are intended to convince men that Jesus is the Christ the Son of God, which is the first step toward becoming a Christian, this book shows what other steps the apostles required them to take. For these reasons, this book which is occupied chiefly with accounts of cases of conversions, is the next book to read after reading the Gospels.

This book also shows how churches were planted and organized by the apostles, and how some very important questions which arose among the disciples were settled; and in these particulars it is our inspiring guide for all time to come. Incidentally it records some of the noblest deeds of the early disciples for our encouragement, and some of the worst for our warning.

Like the Gospels, the book of Acts omits much more than it records; for after a brief account of the activity of all the apostles in Jerusalem, it is occupied for a time with the labors of Peter chiefly, and then, at the thirteenth chapter it assumes the character of a biography by following the labors of the apostle Paul almost exclusively. This last feature was due, from a human point of view, to the fact that the author was more familiar with the labors of Paul than with those of any other apostle; and from the divine point of view, to the fact that Paul's labors, after he became an apostle, were more abundant and more important than those of any other. From the nature of its contents, therefore, we find that the book is not *the* Acts of *the* apostles; but, as the proper form of its title, *Acts of Apostles* indicates, *some* of the acts of *some* of them. How few even of these acts it records, may be inferred from the consideration that though the period which it covers reaches from the resurrection of Christ to the year 63 AD, about thirty years, all is compressed within the limits of a small pamphlet—another instance of the restraining power of the Holy Spirit.

15. The Epistles of Paul

Romans, First Corinthians, Second Corinthians, Galatians, Ephesians, Philippians, Colossians, First Thessalonians, Second Thessalonians, First Timothy, Second Timothy, Titus, Philemon, Hebrews

Paul was not only the greatest of the apostles in the extent of his labors and his sufferings, but he was the most voluminous of all the writers of the New Testament. His writings occupy nearly one-fourth of the whole book. They are not printed in the order in which they were written. They all circulated originally, as did all the books of the New Testament, as separate documents; and when they were collected into larger volumes, they were placed without regard to chronological order.[1] We shall mention their dates, so far as these are known, when speaking of them individually; for it is important, before reading an epistle, to consider who wrote it, when and under what circumstances it was written, and to whom it was addressed.

It is sometimes said by unfriendly writers, that Paul is the real author of Christianity, meaning that he made of that which was first preached a system which had not been intended by Christ. The charge is false, yet in the mind of the great Head of the Church it was allotted to Paul to elaborate, and to set forth much more fully than others did, the divine teachings of Jesus; and also to add much to the revelation of God's will which was first announced by Jesus. No man can, therefore, fully understand the doctrine of

---

[1] The order of the Epistles, in the collection, as of the Prophetic books, was determined not by date of writing, but a larger extent, by size. —W.

Christ without the aid of Paul's exposition of it. Hence the importance to every one of studying carefully his Epistles.

1. *Romans.* Although the Epistle to the Romans was not the first
written by Paul, it is well that it is placed first, and next after Acts;
for its chief subjects is a discussion of the grounds on which a sinner is justified before God, and it is well for the sinner, as soon as
possible after he has turned to the Lord, to be made acquainted
with this subject. Passing out of Acts into Romans is the forward
step which he next needs to take.

This epistle should be read in connection with the twentieth
and twenty-first chapters of Acts, from which the reader can see
that it was written in Corinth just before Paul's last journey to
Jerusalem was begun. Being written to a church containing in its
membership a large number of well matured members with rich
and varied experiences, its discussions of important themes are
more profound than those in any other epistle.

The chief theme of the epistle is the great doctrine of justification by faith. The apostle shows that the ground of our justification
before God is our faith in the Lord Jesus Christ as distinguished
from works of law. He was led to this discussion by the teaching
of certain Jews that we are to be justified by keeping perfectly
the law. To the propounding of his doctrine and the refutation
of objections to it, the apostle devotes the first eleven chapters
of his epistle, and the rest is given to exhortations and the recital
of interesting experiences of himself and others. There are some
things in the doctrinal part which are not adapted to the minds of
children, but all can be read with profit the last part.

2. *First Corinthians.* Some remarks in the last chapter of this epistle, connected with the nineteenth chapter of Acts, show where
the apostle was when he wrote it. The planting of the Corinthian
church is described in the eighteenth chapter of Acts, and these
two chapters in the latter book should be read before beginning
the study of the epistle. Not much information can be obtained
from those about the condition of the church when the epistle was
written; for this we are dependent chiefly on the epistle itself. As

we read the latter, we find, one after another, the circumstances in the condition of the church which called forth the epistle and suggested the topics which it treats. These are all of a practical character, corrective of various kinds of misconduct which had sprung up among the members of this church since Paul had left them. For this reason this is one of the most valuable of all the epistles for the regulation of the life and deportment of a church.

3. *Second Corinthians.* By comparing 1.8–11; 2.12–13; and 8.5–7 of the epistle, with Acts 19.23; 20.1, we learn the place and the circumstances of the apostle when this epistle was written. He had heard through Titus, who is here mentioned for the first time, the effects of his first epistle to the same church, and this information led to the writing of the second. The condition of the church, together with the great peril through which the apostle had just passed in Ephesus, combined very greatly to depress his spirits; and consequently, this is the saddest of all the epistles in the New Testament. It reveals much more fully than any of the other epistles of Paul, or even the thrilling narratives in Acts, the depths of sorrow and suffering through which this great apostle was continually wading in the prosecution of his mission to the Gentiles. The inner life of Paul is more fully revealed here than elsewhere, and this gives the principal value to us of this admirable epistle.[2]

4. *Galatians.* There is little in this epistle to indicate the time or the place at which it was written. The surprise which the writer expresses that the Galatians should have turned so soon away from him to another gospel (1.6), shows that it was written very soon after his last visit, but this is quite indefinite. He had come from Galatia to Ephesus, and after two years and three months there he went through Macedonia to Greece (Acts 18.23; 19.1, 21–22; 20.1–2). Some scholars think that he wrote the epistle while yet in

---

[2]A lost epistle earlier than I Corinthians is mentioned (1 Cor 5.9) and perhaps another lost letter is referred to in 2 Corinthians 2.4; 7.8, which passages do not seem to refer to 1 Corinthians. —W.

Ephesus, which was less than three years from the time he left the Galatians; and others, that he wrote it after he reached Corinth, which was a few months later.

We know nothing of the Galatian churches except what we learn from the epistle; but from this we learn several very interesting facts as to their first reception of Paul and their present relation to him, and also the cause of their present alienation from him. These spring upon the reader of the epistle like flashes of light and sudden darkness, and we shall not anticipate them here.

In opposition to certain false teachers who were nominal Christians and perverters of the truth, Paul teaches here, as in Romans, that the ground of our justification before God is obedient faith, and not works of law. The discussion is brief but conclusive, and he follows it with some admirable and always needed teaching and exhortations on the practical duties of Christian life.

5. *Ephesians*. It is doubtful, to say the least, whether this epistle ought to bear the title which it has; for there is a total absence of those personal greetings which abound in Paul's other epistles addressed to churches which he planted; and this is unaccountable if he was writing to a church with which he had labored more than two years—longer than he stayed with any other. He also speaks of the faith of these brethren as if it was with him a matter of hearsay rather than of personal knowledge (1.15–16); and he refers to his own apostleship to the Gentiles as a matter of hearsay with them, if they had heard it at all (3.1–4). With these indications agrees the fact that in some very early manuscript copies of the epistle the words "at Ephesus" in the salutation (1.1) are not found. It is now most commonly supposed to have been written for a kind of circular letter, and sent to several churches, that at Ephesus among them; and that the name Ephesus got into some early copies from the fact that Ephesus was the principal of the cities for which it was intended. It was written while Paul was a prisoner in Rome (3.1; 4.1; 6.18–20).

The epistle opens with some very grand utterances about the eternal purpose and foreknowledge of God respecting Christ and his work of redemption, and also respecting the call of the Gentiles to be partakers with God's ancient people in his grace. This part closes with the third chapter, and Paul's prayer for the brethren addressed, which closes this chapter, is one of the most impressive passages in all his writings. It should be studied as a model of earnest prayer and lofty sentiment. The remainder of the epistle is of a practical character, having respect to the unity of the church, to its growth in every virtue, and to the details of Christian life on the part of all classes of disciples. Especially remarkable and valuable is the passage in the last chapter, in which the apostle runs a parallel between the pieces of armor worn by an ancient warrior, and the various duties and privileges of a Christian in his struggle against the power of darkness. Fighting and running foot races are favorite illustrations with Paul, because in each, as in the Christian life, a man has to be doing his best all the time to avoid being defeated.

6. *Philippians.* The account of planting the church at Philippi is given in Acts 16.6–40, and it should be read before beginning the study of this epistle. The fact that Paul was in bonds at the time of writing (1.12–13); that the pretorian guard, which was the body guard of the Emperor kept at Rome, had all heard of his preaching (1.13–14); and that he sends to the Philippians the salutation of some belonging to the household of Cæsar (4.22), show very plainly that the epistle was written, as was Ephesians while Paul was a prisoner in Rome. This is the imprisonment mentioned at the close of Acts. The immediate occasion of his writing was the circumstance that a brother named Epaphroditus, having come from Philippi to Rome to bring a contribution for Paul's necessities (4.10–20), had been taken sick, and the Philippians had heard that he was very near the point of death; so Paul sent him back, and doubtless made him the bearer of this epistle (2.19–30). The epistle is full of tender sympathy, and not a word of reproach to the church is found in it, but many words of warm commendation.

7. *Colossians.* This is another of the epistles of the imprisonment, of which there are four, viz: Ephesians, Philippians, Colossians, and Philemon. That Paul was in prison when he wrote is seen from his remarks in 4.2–4, and 4.18. He appears to have sent the epistle by the hand of Tychicus, who also bore Ephesians (4.8; Eph 6.21–22), and this shows that they were both written and forwarded at the same time. This accounts for the fact of a very great similarity between the two epistles, greater than between any other two.

The first chapter of this epistle contains one of the grandest exhibitions of the present glory of our Lord Jesus Christ to be found anywhere in the New Testament. It also abounds in stirring exhortations to Christian activity and zeal, all of which are enforced by the apostle's own example.

8. *First Thessalonians.* In coming to this epistle we turn back in point of time, from Paul's imprisonment mentioned at the close of Acts, to his first visit to Corinth, described in Acts 18.1–18; for it was during that visit that the epistle was written. His labors at Thessalonia are described in Acts 17.1–9. He went thence to Berea (10), thence to Athens (15), and thence to Corinth (18.1). There Silas and Timothy, whom he had left behind, overtook him (18.5); and in the epistle he says: "But when Timothy came even now unto us from you, *etc.;*" which shows that the epistle was written immediately on Timothy's arrival, This, as we learn from the chronology made out from the book of Acts, was in the year 52; and this is the earliest of Paul's epistles, and also the earliest book of the New Testament.[3]

The epistle shows that the Thessalonian church was suffered greatly from persecution, but that it was conducting itself in such a manner as to spread the light of the gospel abroad through surrounding communities (1.2–10). These faithful disciples being but partly instructed in Christian teaching, were in trouble respecting their deceased brethren; and this led Paul to give them one of the

---

[3]Unless, as many scholars think, the epistle of James is to be dated about the year 50 AD, in which case it would be chronologically the first book of the New Testament. —W.

plainest possible lessons about the resurrection of the dead, that by this information they might comfort one another (4.13–18). The same words have been a source of unspeakable comfort to the saints from that day to this, and they have served the purpose of a text on funeral occasions more frequently perhaps than any other passage in the Bible.

9. *Second Thessalonians.* This epistle seems have been written soon after the first to the same church; for the persecution mentioned in the first was still in progress (1.2–3), and the condition of the church in general was unchanged. It was written, too, when the writer was solicitous about being delivered from "unreasonable and evil men," which agrees with the interval between his withdrawal from the synagogue in Corinth to the house of Justus and the assurance given him by the Lord that no one should set on him to harm him (Acts 18.5–10). The most conspicuous matters discussed in it are the fate of the wicked at the second coming of the Lord, and the coming of "the man of sin" here first mentioned by the apostle. It also contains some very plain and emphatic instructions as to how the church should deal with those members who walk disorderly; and in the close shows that Paul always wrote the salutations of his epistles with his own hand as a "token" of their genuineness. He was in the habit, as we have seen from Romans, of dictating his epistles to an amanuensis; but his autograph in the salutation identified them as his.

10. *First Timothy.* When Paul wrote this epistle he had left Timothy in Ephesus and gone into Macedonia (1.3). During that portion of his life covered by Acts of Apostles he had never done this. He had only once gone from Ephesus into Macedonia, and then he had sent Timothy before him (Acts 19.21–22; 20.1). As Acts follows his career until his imprisonment in Rome, where it closes, he must have made the visit to Ephesus here referred to, subsequent to that imprisonment. He must therefore have been released from that imprisonment, as he expected to be, and have gone abroad once more in his apostolic work.

This epistle was especially intended for the instruction of an

Evangelist, which Timothy was, in regard to his labors among the churches. Consequently, it should be studied exhaustively by every preacher of the gospel for his own guidance and edification. But much of the instruction given in it has reference to the duties of church officers; and therefore the epistle is a study for them as well as for preachers. Moreover, the private members of the churches cannot know how to demean themselves toward the officers and the preachers, without knowing what duties and what authorities are imposed upon the latter; therefore it is a study for all church members, having different special aims for different classes. For a knowledge of the practical detail of church organization, we are more dependent on this epistle than on any other.

It would be wise for the student, in connection with this epistle, or with the second to Timothy, to take his concordance and find all the places in which Timothy's name occurs, so as to become familiar with all that is written about him. He is one of the most interesting characters mentioned in the New Testament.

11. *Second Timothy.* Paul is once more a prisoner (1.8, 16–18; 2.9); and it is the imprisonment which terminated in his death (4.6–8, 16–18). It is the last writing which we have from his pen, and this imparts to it that peculiar interest which always attaches to the final utterances of a man of God. It is devoted mostly to personal matters, all the great doctrines of the faith having been set forth in previous documents. The sadness of his situation is indirectly revealed, especially in the first chapter. The exhortations to Timothy, and to all the brethren, in the second chapter, are among the most stirring that Paul ever wrote; and the prediction of a great apostasy which chiefly occupies the third chapter, sounds almost like a wail of despair in regard to the church's future; but the shout of triumph with which he greets his approaching death in the fourth chapter, has thrilled the souls of the saints as scarcely anything else in the Bible. If it so thrills us at the remote period, how must it have inflamed the hearts of Paul's fellow-soldiers and of his thousands of converts! He was anxious to see Timothy once more before he died; he begged him to come to him before winter, and to bring a cloak which he had left at Troas, and which he would need in the fireless prison should cold weather come before his execution. He also wanted something to read, and he thought of doing some more writing; hence the request that Timothy should bring some books and parchments which he had also left at Troas (4.13–21). No one can read this epistle thoughtfully without being better and wiser.

12. *Titus.* But little is known of Titus. He is not once mentioned in Acts; and all that we know of him is found in four of Paul's epistles. He accompanied Paul and Barnabas from Antioch to Jerusalem at the time of the conference on Circumcision (Gal 2.1); he was afterward sent by Paul from Ephesus on an important mission to Corinth (2 Cor 2.12–13; 7.5–7; 9.16–23; 12.18); he was with Paul in the island of Crete after the release of the latter from Roman imprisonment, where he left him to set in order the things that were yet wanting in the churches planted there (Tit 1.5); and he was with Paul in Rome during his last imprisonment, but went thence to Dalmatia before Paul's death (2 Tim 4.10).

He was still in Crete when this epistle was addressed to him (1.5); but was requested by Paul to come to Nicopolis as soon as another evangelist should come to take his place (3.12). The purpose of the epistle is very much the same as that of First Timothy; that is, to instruct Titus as an evangelist in regard to his labors among the churches, and at the same time to impart indirectly the same instruction to the churches. It is a study for young preachers, and not less so for all who would be useful in the church. Its first chapter, in connection with the third chapter of First Timothy, furnishes full instruction with reference to the qualifications required for elders of the church; and as all members are sometimes called upon to act in the selection of these officers, these passages should be familiar to all.

13. *Philemon.* This is one of the epistles of the imprisonment; that is, of the first imprisonment in Rome (1, 13). It was written in behalf of Onesimus, a slave of Philemon, who had run away from his master, had landed in Rome, had turned to the Lord under

Paul's preaching, and for a while had been assisting Paul in his ministry (10–15). Paul broadly suggests to Philemon the propriety of setting him free, and promises to pay out of his own purse anything that Onesimus may owe Philemon (17–21). We learn indirectly from Colossians that Colosse was the home of Onesimus and therefore of Philemon his master. The latter was a man of great benevolence, and of apparent wealth. A church met in his house (2–7).

14. *Hebrews.* This epistle has been generally regarded from the beginning as one of Paul's; but from the second century to the present time many eminent scholars have doubted or denied its Pauline authorship. Three early writers, all born in the second century, but active in the early part of the third, may be regarded as the representatives of the opinions on the question until recent times. Origen said that the thoughts were Paul's, but that the style was not. He was not able to decide who composed it. Clement of Alexandria was of the opinion that Paul wrote it in Hebrew, and that it was translated into Greek by Luke. He thought that the style was Luke's, but the thoughts Paul's. Tertullian ascribed it to Barnabas. In modern time Luther suggested that it might have been written by Apollos, and quite a number of recent scholars have revived and advocated this opinion. Perhaps the question will never be settled to the satisfaction of all. But though opinions may vary as to the person who wrote it, all believing scholars agree that it was written by some apostolic man, and that its contents are to be received a true and authoritative.

The particular community to which it was addressed is left as obscure as the person who wrote it, though it is very clear from the contents that it was primarily intended for a community of Christian Jews, and ultimately for all such and for all believers. It was quite difficult in the first generation of the church to induce the Jews who became Christians to altogether give up those parts of their old religion which were set aside by the new; and some were found who were inclined to go back to Judaism after having accepted the Christian faith. It was for the benefit of these that the epistle was written. Its main line of argument shows the superiority of Christ as a priest over Aaron, and the superiority of his sacrifice of himself over the sacrifices of the law. It shows, indeed, not only the superiority of the former, but the priesthood of Aaron and the sacrifices of the law had been actually set aside to be observed no more. It shows also that all of the ritual of the law which depended on this priesthood and these sacrifices had passed away with them.

While this was the immediate design of the book, its value was not exhausted in its effect on the Jews; for it contains many trains of thought and many practical exhortations which are adapted to all the instruction and edification of all classes of disciples in every age and country. Its exhortations, examples, and warnings, like its chief argument, are drawn almost exclusively from the books of the Old Testament, and no one is prepared to read it intelligibly who is not familiar with those books, and especially with the law of Moses. In studying it one must make almost constant reference, either by memory, or by the marginal references, or by a concordance, to the law books of Moses. Next to the epistle to the Romans, it is generally regarded as the most important epistle in the New Testament for setting forth the distinctive doctrines of Christ.

16. The Catholic Epistles and the Apocalypse

James, First Peter, Second Peter, First John, Second John, Third John, Jude, The Apocalypse

The reader has probably noticed that the first epistle of John, and the epistles of James, Peter and Jude are styled in our printed Testament, "General Epistles." The original of the word "general" is *katholike*, catholic, and from this word these epistles have for a long time been known as the Catholic Epistles. Second and Third John are included in the title, although addressed to individuals, because it was not desirable to classify them separately from the greater epistle by the same author. There are then seven Catholic Epistles, and we shall speak of them in order in which we now find them.

1. *James.* There were three eminent disciples by this name, James the son of Zebedee, James the son of Alphaeus, both apostles; and James the brother of the Lord. For reasons too elaborate to be given here, the last is now very generally understood to be the author of the epistle. From the time of Peter's imprisonment by Herod, which occurred in the year of the Lord 44, till the death of James in the year 62, he seems to have resided continuously in the city of Jerusalem as the acknowledged head of that church in the absence of the apostles (Acts 12.17; 15.13; 21.17–18; Gal 1.18–19; 2.9–12).

The epistle is addressed to "the twelve tribes of the Dispersion," which means those of the twelve tribes dispersed in other countries than Palestine (1.1). The persons addressed, as the contents of the epistle show, were the Christian Jews of the Dispersion, and not the unbelievers. There were very few such Christians until the apostles had been preaching many years, and had made converts in many lands; consequently the date of this epistle must have been near the close of the life of James, but in what year it is now impossible to ascertain.[1] The brethren addressed were suffering persecution, and the purpose of the writer is to encourage them to patient endurance of their afflictions. This purpose pervades the epistle. At the same time many warnings and admonitions are introduced that are appropriate to all times and places. The epistle is especially noted for the most elaborate lesson on the control of the tongue that is to be found in the Bible. It also touches briefly the subject of justification, showing that while, as Paul so abundantly teaches, we are not justified by works of law, yet those works which belong to the obedience of faith are necessary to justification.

This epistle has always been admired for the smoothness and elegance of the style in which it is written, being superior in these particulars to any other New Testament document.

2. *First Peter.* Peter addresses in part the same disciples addressed by James. They are "sojourners of the Dispersion in Pontus, Galatia, Cappadocia, Asia as Bithynia" (1.1). These were provinces in the western and northern parts of what we call Asia Minor, and they were included in the more general Dispersion addressed by James. It was by Paul and his fellow-laborers that these provinces had been evangelized. The main purpose of the epistle is the same as that of James, to encourage these brethren under the persecution which they were enduring, and to prepare them for others that were in their future. Nothing could be better adapted to the purpose than the tender words and earnest appeals which the writer employs. The sentiment throughout reflects a maturity

---

[1]See note on page 86.

of Christian character and experience which make Peter stand before the reader in a far better light than in the Gospels. One familiar with him there could hardly recognize him here—a striking proof of the transforming power of a Christian life.

3. *Second Peter.* In this the apostle addresses the same persons, and mainly for the same purpose (3.1–2). It is chiefly remarkable, however, for two predictions which it contains, the first in the second chapter respecting false teachers who were to arise in the church; and the second, in the third chapter, respecting the coming of Christ to judgment, and the destruction of the present heavens and earth.

Many writers, both ancient and modern, have expressed doubts respecting the genuineness of this epistle; but their arguments have never succeeded in convincing the great mass of believers at any time. From its first to its last word it is worthy the pen of an apostle, and no epistle more positively affirms its own authorship.

4. *First John.* This epistle is not addressed to any particular class of disciples, and it is therefore in the strictest sense catholic or general. After an opening paragraph, in which the writer sets forth very emphatically the fulness of apostolic testimony to the resurrection of Jesus, the epistle is devoted to exhortations to shun sin, and incentives to the love of one another. The latter duty is more persistently set forth here than in any other portion of the New Testament; and this has led to styling the apostle John, The Apostle of Love. He was evidently a very old man when he wrote, for he addresses the disciples of all ages and classes as "Little children," "My little children." This places the epistle among the latest of the New Testament writings, but without fixing its date more definitely. There is some uncertainty whether it or the Gospel of John was the earlier.

5. *Second John.* In this brief note, the writer designates himself by the title, "The Elder." A man, in order to be known by this designation, must have been well known for an age advanced beyond that of any others with whom he was associated. John outlived by very many years all of the other apostles; and before his death he was probably the oldest living member of the church. This would naturally cause everybody to recognize him by this title, and especially all those with whom he was intimate. The chief person addressed in this note, "the elect lady," was a lady not only in our American sense of the word, but in the aristocratic sense of the old world; that is, she was a woman of rank. Such is the meaning of the Greek word rendered lady.

As this lady and her children were not only people of rank, but also of great zeal and hospitality, corrupt men, such as the people call "religious tramps" in our day, got to seeking her hospitality, in order to make use of the fact of having been her guest to impose themselves on others. It was the main purpose of this epistle to caution her on this point. The apostle expected to visit here shortly, and this accounts for the brevity of the epistle. Incidentally, we learn that the epistle was written, not on parchment, but on paper. It was probably very soon copied on more enduring material or it might have perished.

6. *Third John.* Another brief note from "The Elder," addressed to a brother named Gaius, who seems to have been as much noted in the church as the "elect lady" of the second epistle, and for the same excellent qualities. He was particularly liberal in "forwarding on their way" such brethren as passed by him on their way to distant fields of labor. The purpose of the epistle was to commend him for this, and to warn him against a certain brother named Diotrephes, who "loved to have the pre-eminence," and had lifted himself up against even the authority of the apostle. He lets Gaius understand that he will deal with this reprobate according to his deserts when he visits that church. He has much to say to Gaius as he had to the "elect lady," but defers it until he can speak "face to face."

These two personal notes are of great value in that they throw light at once upon the loving relations existing between the aged apostle and his faithful to co-laborers, both men and women, and upon the unruly conduct of unconverted or half converted men who even then had crept into the churches. This last circumstance prevents us from being surprised or disheartened when we see the same thing in our own day.

7. *Jude.* The real name of this writer, as we see from the first verse of the epistle, was Judas. The English translators probably adopted the improper name Jude, to prevent ignorant persons from thinking that it was Judas Iscariot. He calls himself "the brother of James," and it is now commonly believed among scholars that he means, brother of that James who was a brother of the Lord. If this is correct, he also was a brother of the Lord; but as the Lord had ascended to Heaven, it was more becoming to call himself brother of James than brother of the Lord. He declares it to be the purpose of his epistle to exhort the brethren to contend earnestly for the faith once for all delivered to the saints, in view of the fact that many bad men had crept into the churches who were corrupting both the faith and the morals of the brethren. His denunciations of these characters remind us of some of the similar denunciations of bad men by the Old Testament prophets, and of our Lord's denunciations of the hypocritical scribes and Pharisees. They resemble still more the second chapter of 2 Peter. He reminds the brethren that the apostles had predicted the appearance of such men, and that their coming was therefore not a matter of surprise. He closes with a benediction which is one of the most beautiful and appropriate to be found in any literature.

8. *The Apocalypse.* The word apocalypse means revelation; but as other books as well as this contain revelations, there is a little confusion in calling this the book of revelation; hence the preference among scholars for the untranslated title. There is still another objection to the printed title, "The Revelation of St. John the Divine"; for John was no more a saint, and no more a divine than any of the other apostles. The real title of the book, that is, the one given by the writer himself, is found in the first verse; "The revelation of Jesus Christ which God gave him to show unto his servants, even the things which must shortly come to pass; and he went and signified it by his angel unto his servant John, who

bore witness of the word of God, and of the Testimony of Jesus Christ, even of all things that he saw." As it was intended to show "things which must shortly come to pass," its contents must be in the main prophetic.

This fully stated title is followed by a salutation to the "Seven churches of Asia," similar to the usual salutation of the epistles, and this by a doxology. Then the main body of the book opens with an account of the appearance to John on the island of Patmos, of the Lord Jesus himself in glory. The Lord commands him to write what he dictates, and there follow seven brief epistles from the Lord to the seven churches of Asia. The word Asia means the Roman province of which Ephesus was the principal city. By consulting any good map the reader will find the seven churches, or rather the cities in which they were located, almost in a circle. If this book was written about the year 96, as Irenaeus, a writer of the second century affirms, Jesus had now been in heaven about sixty-two years, and these seven churches had been in existence nearly forty years.[2] After the experience of this long period the Lord dictates a letter to each of them to let them know how he regarded their conduct since they were planted, and to give them warnings and exhortations for the future. When the epistle to each was publicly read to the assembled members, the occasion must have been one never to be forgotten. In reading them we should keep in mind a comparison with our own congregation, and so far as the conditions are similar we should take to ourselves the same warnings, or commendations, as the case may be.

After writing the words of the seven epistles as they fell from the lips of the Lord, John saw in a vision a door opened in heaven, and at the bidding of a voice he was caught up through it, and beheld a vision of the glory of God far transcending any vouchsafed before to any prophet or apostle. Then followed a vision of a book sealed with seven seals, which no one in heaven was

---

[2]Many scholars believe the date of the apocalypse to have been about 68 AD, shortly after the Neronian persecution, and during the earlier stages of the Jewish war, which culminated in the fall of Jerusalem (70 AD). This would make the apocalypse the earliest of the writings of John.—W.

found worthy to unseal except "The Lion of the Tribe of Judah," a well known title of our Lord Jesus Christ. When he took the book in his hand great glory was ascribed to him by all the inhabitants of heaven; and as he proceeded to open the seven seals there followed the opening of each a wonderful symbolic vision portending something to occur on earth (4.1–7.17). When the seventh seal was opened seven angels stood forth with seven trumpets in their hands. They sounded their trumpets one by one, and there followed as many startling events (8.1–11.19). The rest of the book (12–22) is filled with a series of visions of quite a different character and too elaborate for description here, all terminating with a vision of the final judgment and of the New Jerusalem in which the saints are to dwell in the presence of God forever. Thus the Bible, which began with a vision of the creation of the present heavens and earth, in which sin was born and the Redeemer from sin was crucified, closes with a vision of a new heaven and a new earth where those redeemed from sin out of every nation, family and tongue, shall live perpetually in righteousness and bliss. The promise to Abraham has never been lost sight of since it was first announced in Ur of the Chaldees, and it is now fulfilled by the blessing which comes upon men of all nations through Abraham's seed.

17. A Brief Review

The student who has followed us through this little book can now look back and see the Bible as no one can see it who has not pursued a similar course of study. He can plainly see, that there was a long period, that from Adam to Moses, when no part of our Bible was in existence, but when faithful men served God as best they could without a book to guide them. This period is called the Patriarchal Age of the World; and the system of religious faith and practice then in force, the Patriarchal Dispensation of Religion. The only established rites were sacrifice and prayer, until in Abraham's family circumcision was added. Every head of the family acted as a priest for his own household. They were not without such a a knowledge of God's will as justified speaking of his "commandments, his statutes, and his law" (Gen 26.5). These must have been very simple and elementary compared with the legislation which followed; yet under them were developed such men of faith as Abel, Enoch, Noah, Abraham, Job, and others. If we wish to know what the Patriarchal religion was, we look for it to the book of Genesis and the book of Job as our chief sources of information; and secondarily to remarks on the subject of that religion to be found here and there in other books; but no one with any knowledge of the Bible would look there to find how to become a Christian and to love the life which Christ now requires.

The reader can see, in the second place, that the form of religion instituted by God through Moses began with that prophet and continued until the public ministry of Christ. Under it many rites and ceremonies were added to the primitive prayer and sacrifice, and a new priesthood was appointed, the privilege of offering sacrifice, except under extraordinary circumstances, being limited to Aaron and his sons, and the places of offering being limited to those in which God would "place his name," or would appoint as the proper place from time to time. This was the Jewish dispensation, and it intervened between the Patriarchal and the Christian. If, then, one desires to know what religious ordinances characterized the Jewish religion, or what, in any particular, a man had to do to please God under that dispensation, he must go to the law of Moses, and to the examples of good men set forth in other Old Testament books than Job and Genesis. The ideas of God and of duty which regulated the lives of good men then are in the main the same which should regulate ours; but, as we have seen, there were many differences, sentiments and acts that were then thought to be right being known by us to be wrong. We cannot therefore take the teachings and examples of the Old Testament books as our guide, except so far as they agree with what we are taught in the New.

In the third place, the reader can see that the New Testament introduces an order of things in the service of God that is in many respects entirely new. It requires faith in Jesus Christ, which was not required before; and the baptism which it requires, is unknown to the Old Testament. Remission of sins is offered to the penitent in the name of Jesus, churches are organized for worship and instruction, the death of the Lord is commemorated by a new ordinance styled the Lord's supper; preachers are sent out everywhere to bring sinners to repentance and obedience; and a purer system of morals than was ever known on earth before is enjoined on all men. Finally, the hope of heaven and the fear of hell are held out before men in a clear light unknown before. All this is the result of having now a new high priest who has taken the place of Aaron's sons, and a new sacrifice for sins in his death as our atonement. He has been made the head of all things for the church, and the judge of the living and the dead.

If now a man under the present dispensation wishes to know what to believe in order to be saved, and where to find the evidence on which to rest his faith, he must go, not to Genesis, to Leviticus, to the Psalms, or to the Prophets, where he would learn only Patriarchalism or Judaism, but to the four Gospels which were written that we may believe that Jesus Christ is the Son of God, and that believing we may obtain life through him (John 21.20–21). After being thus led to believe in Jesus, we must next read the book of Acts, which was written to teach us how believers were brought into the churches, receiving the forgiveness of their sins and a place among the redeemed. Here we find the cases of conversion which were directed by the inspired apostles, and were put on record as models for men in all time to come. Having compiled with the requirements here found, and become disciples of Christ in the full sense of the word, the epistles are next studied that a fuller knowledge may be obtained of the duties and privileges that pertain to a Christian life, and a more profound knowledge of the great principles of the divine government in accordance with which a sinner has attained to a condition so exalted.

During the course of these studies the young disciple will have caught many glimpses of the glory and bliss yet to be revealed in the faithful, and on reading the last book of the Bible he sees broader and grander visions of the heavenly glory than he could have conceived before; and although many of the visions of rapture and of terror which pass before him are but imperfectly understood, he realizes all the more from this that the final fate of the wicked on the one hand, is wretched beyond conception, and that the bliss and glory of the saints rises far above the reach of human thought while in the flesh. Thus ends the book of God; and thus will end the life of every one who patiently learns its heavenly lessons and faithfully follows its infallible guidance.

Questions

Chapter 1
Define, as to origin and use, the words Bible, Testament, Scriptures, Oracles.

Chapter 2
What are the names and number of books in the Pentateuch? the historical group? the poetic or wisdom group? the prophetic division?

Chapter 3
1. In what language was the most of the Old Testament written? 2. What was the earliest means of multiplying the Scriptures? 3. How might mistakes occur? 4. What method was employed to prevent this? 5. What change was effected by printing? 6. What proof that we have the genuine books of the Old Testament?

Chapter 4
a. *Genesis.* 1. How did the first Old Testament book receive its present name? 2. With what do the first eleven chapters deal? 3. What single character is next described? 4. Why is Abraham important in the history? 5. What promises were made to Abraham? 6. What descendants of Abraham are described in the remaining part of Genesis? 7. How long a period is covered by the events of this book?

b. *Exodus.* 1. What was the condition of Israel in Egypt? 2. What gives the book its title? 3. How and by whom were they delivered?

4. Describe the giving of the law and the building of the Tabernacle?

c. *Leviticus.* 1. To what subject is this book devoted? 2. How did it receive its name? 3. What kinds of sacrifices are enumerated in it?

d. *Numbers.* 1. How is this title appropriate to the book? 2. How long and at what places were the people in the wilderness? 3. What nations were conquered? 4. What is recorded of Balaam?

e. *Deuteronomy.* 1. Meaning of the title? 2. Why given? 3. Where is the scene laid? 4. What were the cities of refuge? 5. What is the substance of the blessings and curses? 6. What events were connected with the death of Moses?

Make a list of the qualities of God's nature which were most impressively revealed by the experiences of this period.

Chapter 5

a. *Joshua.* 1. Why is this book so named? 2. What is the theme of the book? 3. Make a list of the battles recorded. 4. A list of the miracles. 5. Compare the character of Joshua with that of Moses in five particulars.

b. *Judges.* 1. From what does the book take its name? 2. What was the condition of the country as to (a) government, (b) relation of the Israelites to the Canaanites, (c) morals and religion? 3. How many Judges are described? 4. From what tribes do they come? 5. What did they accomplish? 6. How long a period is covered by this book?

c. *Ruth.* 1. With what book is this closely connected and yet in striking contrast? 2. What are the leading features of the narrative? 3. What were its purposes?

d. *First Samuel.* 1. Describe Samuel's parentage, early life, call and the prophecy regarding Eli's house. 2. What events led to Eli's death? 3. How was the first king chosen? 4. What were the leading elements in his character? 5. Describe the decline of Saul and the rise of David. 6. Analyze Samuel's character and influence in seven particulars.

e. *Second Samuel.* 1. Did Samuel write these books? 2. Who are the leading characters in this book? 3. What were the leading events in David's life? 4. What were the consequences of David's great sin? 5. What literary activity was begun during this period? 6. What prophets are mentioned?

Chapter 6

1. How was Solomon seated on the throne? 2. What was his choice? 3. What was the chief event of his reign? 4. What were the characteristics of Solomon's reign as to (1) prosperity, (2) extent of dominion, (3) commerce, (4) court splendor, (5) taxation, (6) literary activity? 5. What was the sin of Solomon's later years? 6. What was the cause of the division of the kingdom?

Chapter 7

1. What two kingdoms followed the united kingdom of Solomon? 2. In what books is this part of the history recorded? 3. What false worship did Jeroboam establish? 4. Name the kings of the Northern Kingdom (Israel). 5. Those of the Southern (Judah). 6. What great prophet arose? 7. What marriage reconciled the two kingdoms? 8. Describe the characteristics of (1) Ahab, (2) Jezebel, (3) Jehoshaphat, (4) Athaliah, (5) Jehu, (6) Elijah, (7) Elisha. 9. What heathen worship prevailed in the Northern Kingdom? 10. What descendant of Jehu enjoyed the most prosperous reign? 11. What foreign wars were waged during all this time? 12. What prophets lived in the time of Jeroboam II? 13. Describe the decline and fall of Israel. 14. In what year and by whom was it overthrown?

Chapter 8

1. In what books is the story of the surviving kingdom of Judah told? 2. What was the character of the reign of (1) Jotham, (2) Ahaz, (3) Hezekiah, (4) Manasseh, (5) Josiah? 3. What may be said of the date and prophetic work of (1) Isaiah, (2) Jeremiah? 4. What were the occasion and character of the reformation under Josiah? 5. What was its success?

Chapter 9

1. What was the date of Micah? (See list of prophets in appendix). 2. What were the subjects on which he spoke? 3. Against what city did Nahum speak? 4. Date and theme of Habakkuk's prophecy? 5. The subject of his prayer? 6. Date of Zephaniah and his relation to the reformation of Josiah? 7. Against what people did Obadiah speak, and for what crime? 8. Where and when did Ezekiel live? 9. Name some of symbols and visions of this book. 10. With what especially does the closing part deal? 11. What kind of a scourge does Joel describe? 12. What beautiful prophecy does he record?

Chapter 10

a. *Job.* 1. How are the so-called prophetical books to be classified? 2. What is the theme of the book of Job? 3. What are its characters? 4. Name some of its most striking descriptions. 5. Is the book to be regarded as (1) fiction, (2) literal history, or (3) poetic elaboration of a real experience?

b. *Psalms.* 1. How many books of Psalms are there? 2. Who was the author of many of these Psalms? 3. Do the Psalms come from one period of the history, or several? 4. What events in David's life may have been the occasion for Psalms? 5. What other authors are named in the book? 6. Of what are the Psalms the record?

c. *Proverbs.* 1. What is the character of the book of Proverbs? 2. What are its leading divisions? 3. What was Solomon relation to it? 4. What other persons are named as authors or collectors? 5. What is the chief value of the book?

d. *Ecclesiastes.* 1. What is the meaning of the title? 2. Who is made the subject of the book? 3. What may be said of its authorship? 4. What is the purpose of the book?

e. *Song of Songs.* 1. What is the literary character of this book? 2. Who are the leading persons? 3. What different views may be given of its value and its right to a place in the Bible?

Chapter 11

1. What is meant by the exile? 2. Who was Daniel? 3. How did he

come to be in Babylon? 4. What are the leading events recorded in the book? 5. What was the purpose of their narration? 6. With what events does the book of Esther deal? 7. What are its leading characters? 8. What was probably the purpose? 9. What other literary materials belong to the same period?

Chapter 12

a. *Ezra.* 1. Of what is this book the continuation? 2. What events does it record? 3. What great enterprise engaged the people after the return from exile? 4. What hindrances arose? 5. Under whose direction was the Temple completed? 6. How was the law enforced?

b. *Nehemiah.* 1. With what other writing was the book originally connected? 2. What were Nehemiah's office and experience in Persia? 3. What did he do after arrival in Jerusalem? 4. Describe his visit to Babylon and return.

c. *Haggai.* 1. What were the date and duration of this prophet's work? 2. To what enterprise did he encourage the people? 3. What did he say were the results of their failure in this duty?

d. *Zechariah.* 1. How was the work of this prophet related to that of Haggai? 2. With what other themes than the rebuilding of the Temple is the book concerned?

e. *Malachi.* 1. What is the date of this prophet? 2. What sins does he rebuke? 3. What promises and predictions does he make?

What are the Apocryphal books of the Old Testament? (See list in Appendix). What is their value? With what period do they deal?

Chapter 13

1. What are the divisions of the New Testament? 2. How many books in each? (See introduction.) 3. What are the characteristics of (1) the Gospels, (2) Acts, (3) the Epistles, (4) the Apocalypse?

Chapter 14

a. *Matthew.* 1. What is known of the author? 2. How does he introduce Jesus? 3. Why does he make use of the Old Testament? 4. With what part of Jesus' work does the book largely deal? 5. What are the general divisions of the book? 6. Make a list of its (1) discourses, (2) parables, (3) miracles. 7. To whom was it especially addressed?

b. *Mark.* 1. What is known of Mark? 2. From what apostle is it probable he received directions in the preparation of the book? 3. How is this indicated? 4. What is the purpose of the book? 5. Which element in Jesus' work is largely recorded? 6. To what type of mind would the book specially commend itself? 7. Compare the list of miracles with Matthew's.

c. *Luke.* 1. How account for the similarities found in these three Gospels? 2. The differences? 3. Where do all these Gospels lay the scene of most of Jesus' work? 4. What are the divisions of Luke's Gospel? 5. What do we know of the author? 6. To whom is the book addressed? 7. Compare the parables and discourses with those in Matthew. 8. What is the probable date of its composition? (See table in appendix).

d. *John.* 1. By what name are the first three Gospels known? 2. Why? 3. How does John's differ from them? 4. What data are given by John, but omitted by the others? 5. What are the characteristics of John's Gospel? 6. What is its value among the books of the New Testament?

e. *Acts.* 1. Who is its author? 2. Probable date? (See table in appendix). 3. What forms the theme of the book? 4. Give an outline of its leading events. 5. With what apostle's work is the first part concerned? 6. The second part? 7. Make a list of its (1) leading persons, (2) discourses, (3) miracles, (4) places. 8. What were the requirements for membership in the church as disclosed by this book?

Chapter 15

1. In what particulars did Paul surpass the other apostles? 2. What was the relation which Paul bore to Christ and Christianity? 3. What determined the order of the Epistles?

a. *Romans.* 1. How many chapters in this book? 2. At what period in Paul's life was it written? (See outline in appendix). 3. What is the great subject of this epistle? 4. What gave rise to the necessity for such an epistle? 5. In what chapters of the book are to be found (1) a terrible sketch of the sin of heathenism, (2) the grounds of Justification by Faith, (3) the confidence of Paul, (4) the great lessons of practical Christian life?

b. *First Corinthians.* 1. What were the date and place at which this book was written? 2. What were the facts regarding the founding of the church at Corinth? 3. What is shown to have been the condition of the church in the matter of (1) divisions, (2) disorders at the Lord's Supper, (3) other troubles in the church? 4. What is the most beautiful chapter in the book, perhaps in the Bible?

c. *Second Corinthians.* 1. How long after the first letter to Corinth was this sent? 2. What may be learned from it regarding Paul's opposers? 3. In what respect is this the most personal epistle Paul ever sent? 4. Were there other epistles to the church at Corinth now lost?

d. *Galatians.* 1. Where were the Galatian churches? 2. What may be said as to the date and place of this writing? 3. For what does Paul reprove the Galatians? 4. How is salvation to be secured?

e. *Ephesians.* 1. What doubts may be thrown on the title of this book? 2. When was the book written? 3. What is the general theme? 4. In what chapter is found (1) the statement as to the means of progress in the Christian life, (2) the model prayer, (3) the description of the Christian armor?

f. *Philippians.* 1. Where is the account of the planting of this church? 2. Where was Paul at the time of writing? 3. What was the occasion of its being written? 4. What persons was Paul going to send to Philippi? 5. Where is the passage regarding (1) the humiliation of Christ, (2) Paul's thoughts of life and death, (3) the model discipline?

g. *Colossians.* 1. What were the four epistles of the first imprisonment of Paul? 2. Where was Colosse? 3. What are some of the leading characters of this epistle?

h. *First Thessalonians.* 1. How does this epistle stand in the order of Paul's writings? 2. What events had transpired at Thessalonica? 3. What had occurred to trouble some of the disciples there? 4. What is the teaching of Paul on the subject of the resurrection?

i. *Second Thessalonians.* 1. What are the indications as to time? 2. What theme is uppermost in the epistle? 3. What are the practical instructions?

j. *First Timothy.* 1. Who was Timothy? 2. Where is he mentioned in Acts? 3. When was this epistle written? 4. What was the work of Timothy? 5. What workers in the church may especially profit by the teachings of this epistle?

k. *Second Timothy.* 1. What is Paul's condition at this writing? 2. How does this epistle stand in the order of Paul's letters? 3. What does the Apostle say regarding his approaching death? 4. What request did he make of Timothy?

l. *Titus.* 1. What is known of Titus? 2. In what duties does the epistle instruct him?

m. *Philemon.* 1. To which group of Paul's epistles does this belong? 2. What persons are mentioned? 3. What is the request made of Philemon?

n. *Hebrews.* 1. Is this regarded as an epistle of Paul? 2. Who have been suggested as possible authors? 3. What is the probable date? 4. How does it represent the relation of Christianity to Judaism? 5. Where in it is to be found (1) the comparison of Aaron's priesthood with that of Christ, (2) the statement regarding Melchizedek, (3) the roll call of the heroes of the faith?

Chapter 16

1. What is meant by Catholic epistles? 2. How many are there? 3. Why are II John and III John included in this list?

a. *James.* 1. Which James was the author of this book? 2. To whom is the book addressed? 3. What was the probable date of its composition? 4. What was the purpose? 5. What does it say regarding (1) the tongue, (2) pure religion, (3) faith and works?

b. *First Peter.* 1. Where did the Christians addressed in this epistle live? 2. What does the apostle say regarding (1) the Word of God, (2) the corner stone, (3) baptism, (4) probability of persecution?

c. *Second Peter.* 1. What does the writer say of things to be "added?" 2. Of the transfiguration of Christ? 3. What warnings are uttered?

d. *First John.* 1. What is the order of John's writings. (See table in the appendix). 2. What is the chief duty set forth in this epistle? 3. How does John address his readers? 4. Enumerate five points in the teachings of this epistle?

e. *Second John.* 1. To whom was this letter addressed? 2. For what purpose?

f. *Third John.* 1. What kind of a man does the epistle show Gaius to have been? 2. What is the value of these two brief letters?

g. *Jude.* 1. Who was the author of this writing? 2. What was the object of the epistle? 3. Why was this needed?

h. *The Apocalypse.* 1. What is the meaning of this word? 2. In what place among John's writings does the book probably come? 3. Where was the author? 4. What seems to have been the purpose of the book? 5. What relation do the scenes and visions of the book bear to the events of the time; such as the persecution of the Christians by Nero and the destruction of Jerusalem? 6. What is John's confidence as to the final issue of the struggle between the forces of evil and the church?

Chapter 17

1. What characterized the patriarchal age? 2. The Mosaic age? 3. The Christian age? 4. What is the right division of the Scriptures? 5. What is the purpose of (1) the Gospels, (2) Acts, (3) the Epistles, (4) the Apocalypse?

Appendixes

1. Early Translations of the Scriptures

2. Translations of the Scriptures into English

3. Extra Canonical Books

4. Outline of the History of Israel

5. Leading Prophets of the Old Testament

6. Important Events in the Life of Christ

7. Outline of the Journeys and Labors of Paul

8. Chronological Order of New Testament Books

The following material is added for convenient reference on the part of the reader. It is purely outline in character, treating in brief terms of subjects on which every Bible student desires hints. Much other material might have been added, but it was thought desirable to widen the bounds of this part of the book. —W.

Appendix 1

Early Translations of the Scriptures

1. The Septuagint (LXX) translation of the Old Testament into Greek. Begun about 250 BC

2. Translations of portions of the Old Testament into Greek by Aquila and Theodotian, Second century AD

3. The Targums, free translations of the Old Testament into the popular language, the Aramaic, Second century

4. The Old Latin Bible, Old and New Testaments (Second century) out of which came the Vulgate of Jerome, the text used in the Roman Catholic Church

5. An Ancient Syriac Version, Second century

6. Two Egyptian Versions in different dialects, Third century.

7. Peshito-Syriac, Fourth century

8. Gothic Version, Fourth century

9. Ethiopic Version, Fourth century

10. Armenian Version, Fifth century

Appendix 2
Translations of the Scriptures into English

1. A paraphrase in poetry by Cædmon of Whitby, 680 AD
2. Two versifications of the Psalms, about 700
3. The Gospel of John by Venerable Bede, finished May 27, 735
4. Exodus and the Psalms, Alfred the Great, 901
5. Two interlinear translations of portions of the Scriptures from the Latin Vulgate, about 950
6. A translation of the greater part of the Bible into Norman French, 1260
7. Four versions of the Psalms, and parts of the New Testament, 1350
8. John Wyclif; the first complete translation into English from the Vulgate; New Testament completed in 1380, the Old Testament in 1384
9. Tyndale; the first translation from the original Hebrew and Greek, 1525–1536
10. Coverdale; the first complete Bible ever *printed*. It was based on the Vulgate, Luther's German Bible, and Tyndale, 1535
11. Matthew's (really Roger's) Bible. The first authorized version, 1537
12. Crammer's, or the Great Bible, 1539
13. The Geneva Bible, published by the English exiles in Geneva, the first Bible with chapter and verse divisions, based on the Vulgate, 1557–1560
14. The Bishop's Bible, 1564–1568
15. The Authorized, or King James Version, 1611
16. The Revised Version; New Testament, 1881; Old Testament, 1884

Appendix 3
Extra Canonical Books

In addition to the books that have been generally recognized among Protestants as worthy of a place in the Canon, or collection of Sacred books, which taken as a whole makes up the Bible, there are certain other books which had their origin in the period beginning after the time of Malachi, and closing with the Christian century. They are called the apocryphal books of the Old Testament, and while regarded by the Roman Catholic Church as having a place in the Canon, and by many Protestants as containing much profitable reading, their value is clearly below that of the books included in our Canon. They are as follows:

1 Maccabees
2 Maccabees
Judith
Tobit
Psalms of Solomon
Esdras
Baruch
Ecclesiasticus, or the Wisdom of Jesus the Son of Sirach
Prayer of the Three Children, Susanna, and Bel and the Dragon (apocryphal additions to the Book of Daniel)
The Prayer of Manasseh
The Wisdom of Solomon
The Epistle of Jeremiah

A similar class of literature grew up subsequently to the writings of the New Testament and connected with it. Among books of this class may be named the following:

The Apocryphal Gospels
The Shepherd of Hermes
The Epistles of Clement to the Corinthians
Epistle of Barnabas
Paul and Thecala

Appendix 4
Outline of the History of Israel

The purpose of this outline is to give only the general features of the History of Israel and their dates as nearly as they can be ascertained.

1. Patriarchal Period: Abraham, Isaac, Jacob, Joseph, The Bondage (2000–1500 BC are the approximate limits of this period.)

2. Exodus, Conquest and Establishment in Canaan: Moses, Joshua, the Judges, Samuel (1500–1050 BC)

3. The United Kingdom: Saul, David, Solomon (1050–937 BC)

4. Israel and Judah
   a. Revolt of the Ten Tribes (937 BC)
   b. Reformation under Jehu (842 BC)
   c. Destruction of Samaria (721 BC)
   d. Captivity of Judah (586 BC)

5. The Exile in Babylon (586–534 BC)

6. The Restoration: Zerubbabel, Jeshua, Ezra, Nehemiah (534–400 BC)
   a. Temple founded (534 BC)
   b. Work stopped (522 BC)
   c. Temple completed (515 BC)
   d. Ezra's arrival (459 BC)
   e. Arrival of Nehemiah (433 BC)
   f. His second arrival (425 BC)

7. Greek and Syrian rule (333–166 BC)
   a. Greek rule, Alexander (333–320 BC)
   b. Egyptian rule, the Ptolemies (320–314 BC)
   c. Syrian rule, the Selucidae (314–166 BC)

8. The Maccabees; the struggle for liberty; Judas Maccabaeus, Jonathan, Simon, John Hyrcanus, Aristobulus, Alexander Jannaeus, Alexandra (166–63 BC)

9. Roman Dominion (63 BC–70 AD)
   a. Jerusalem taken by Pompey (63 BC)
   b. Maccabean governors (63–47 BC)
   c. Antipater, Roman Procurator (46–41 BC)
   d. Herod the Great, his son, tributary king (40–4 BC)
   e. Herods and Procurators (4 BC–70 AD)
   f. Destruction of Jerusalem by Romans and end of Jewish state (70 AD)

Appendix 5
Leading Prophets of the Old Testament

The approximate dates at which they lived are as follows: Moses (1500 BC); Samuel (1050); Elijah (875); Elisha (850); Jonah (770); Amos (760); Hosea (740); Isaiah (725); Micah (715); Nahum (660); Zephaniah (640); Habakkuk (610); Jeremiah (600); Obadiah (586); Ezekiel (585); Daniel (550); Haggai (525); Zechariah (525); Malachi (475); Joel (400?).

Appendix 6
Important Events in the Life of Christ

1. Preparatory Period (4 BC–26 AD)
   a. Birth of Jesus (4 BC)
   b. Jesus in the Temple (8 AD)
   c. Life in Nazareth (8–26 AD)
2. Early Ministry, Judea (26–27 AD)
   a. Baptism, Temptation, First Disciples
   b. Visit to Cana and Capernaum
   c. First Passover, Nicodemus
3. Period of popular favor; Galilee (27–29 AD)
   a. John imprisoned; Samaria; Galilee
   b. Rejection at Nazareth
   c. Twelve chosen
   d. Sermon on the Mount
   e. Tours through Galilee; Parables and Miracles
   f. Five thousand fed. The Bread of Life
4. Period of Opposition; Galilee, Judea and Perea (29–30 AD)
   a. The Great Confession; the Transfiguration
   b. Departure from Galilee; the Seventy sent out
   c. Lazarus raised; retirement to Perea.
   d. Return to Jerusalem; teachings on the way; Jericho, Zacchaeus; arrival at Bethany
5. The Final Week; Jerusalem (30 AD)
   a. Triumphal entry.
   b. Teaching and controversies in the Temple
   c. Greeks at the feast; Discourse on the Last Days
   d. The Passover; the Last Supper; Gethsemane
   e. Arrest; examination; crucifixion; burial
6. Resurrection and Ascension (30 AD)
   a. Resurrection; appearances to the Disciples
   b. Meetings with the Disciples in Galilee; forty days
   c. The Ascension

Appendix 7
Outline of the Journeys and Labors of the Apostle Paul

1. Preparation
   (1) Birth and Early Life at Tarsus, Acts 21.39; 22.3
   (2) Education at Jerusalem, Acts 22.3
   (3) Saul the Persecutor, Acts 8.1–3; 12.4; 26.11; Galatians 1.13, 23; 1 Corinthians 15.9; Philippians 3.6; 1 Timothy 1.13
   (4) The Conversion, Acts 9.3–19; 20.6–16; 26.12–18. (35 AD)
   (5) Arabia, Galatians 1.17
   (6) The return to Tarsus (38–43 AD)
       (a) Damascus, Acts 9.19–25
       (b) Jerusalem, Acts 9.26–30.
       (c) Tarsus, Galatians 1.21; Acts 9.30

2. The First Period of Missionary Activity (44–51 AD)
   (1) Antioch the second center of Christianity, Acts 9.19–26
   (2) Famine in Jerusalem, Relief from Antioch, Acts 11.27–12.25
   (3) The First Missionary Journey, with Barnabas; Cyprus; Antioch of Pisidia; Iconium; Lystra; Derbe; the return, Acts 13.1–14.28
   (4) The Consultation at Jerusalem, Acts 15.1–35

3. The Second Period of Missionary Activity (51–54 AD)
   (1) Separation of Paul and Barnabas, Acts 15.36–40
   (2) The second Missionary Journey, with Silas; Galatia; Troas; Philippi; Thessalonica; Berea; Athens, Acts 15.41–17.34
   (3) Residence at Corinth, eighteen months, Acts 18.1–17
   (4) 1 Thessalonians and 2 Thessalonians written during this stay in Corinth (52–53 AD)
   (5) Return to Antioch via Ephesus and Jerusalem, Acts 18.18–23

4. The Third Period of Missionary Activity (54–58 AD)
   (1) Return to Ephesus from Antioch, Acts 18.23–19.1

(2) Galatians written (c. 55 AD)

(3) Residence in Ephesus three years, Acts 19.1–20.1

(4) 1 Corinthians written (57 AD)

(5) Journey via Troas to Macedonia, Acts 20.1–2;
2 Corinthians 2.12–13

(6) 2 Corinthians written (57 AD)

(7) Second visit to Corinth, three months, Acts 20.2–3

(8) Romans written at Corinth (57 or 58 AD)

(9) Return to Jerusalem via Troas, Miletus, Tyre, Caesarea,
Acts 20.3–21.16

5. The Period of Imprisonment (58–63 AD)

(1) Arrest in Jerusalem, Acts 21.17–23.35. (Pentecost, 58 AD)

(2) Imprisonment in Cæsarea, Acts 24.1–26.32. (58–60 AD)

(3) The Voyage to Rome, Acts 27.1–28.16

(4) Imprisoned in Rome, Acts 28.16–31. (61–63 AD)

(5) Epistles of the First Roman Imprisonment; Philippians,
Colossians, Philemon, Ephesians (62–63 AD)

6. The Last Period; Conjectural (63–66 AD)

(1) Probable release; Journey to Spain (?)

(2) Ephesus, Macedonia, Crete, Troas

(3) 1 Timothy and Titus written

(4) Second Arrest, and return to Rome

(5) 2 Timothy written

(6) Martyrdom

Appendix 8
Chronological Order of the Books of the New Testament

While no arrangement of these books can be made with absolute confidence, the following dates are sufficiently reliable to serve the purpose of the Bible student.

James, 50 AD

1 Thessalonians, 52–53

2 Thessalonians, 52–53

Galatians, 55

1 Corinthians, 57

2 Corinthians, 57

Romans, 57–58

Philippians, 62–63

Colossians, 62–63

Philemon, 62–63

Ephesians, 62–63

Luke, 63

Acts, 64

1 Timothy, 65

Titus, 65

2 Timothy, 66

Mark, 66

Matthew, 67

Hebrews, 67

1 Peter, 67–68

II Peter, 68

Jude, 68

Apocalypse, 68

John, c. 85

Epistles of John, 90–95

Also from DeWard Publishing
Heritage of Faith Library

The Man of Galilee
Atticus G. Haygood

Dr. Haygood's apologetic for the deity of Christ using Jesus Himself as presented by the gospel records as its chief evidence. This is a reprint of the 1963 edition. The Man of Galilee was originally published in 1889. 108 pages. $8.99.

Jesus and Jonah
J.W. McGarvey

McGarvey's defense of the historicity of the Biblical account of the book of Jonah based on Jesus' teaching about Jonah—which is the same as His teaching regarding the historicity of the rest of the Old Testament. This would indicate that Jesus either accepts all of it as historical or none of it as historical. Since the New Testament makes it plain that Jesus accepts the Old as historical, McGarvey argues that the denial of the Jonah story makes Jesus either a liar or a fool.

A Treatise on the Eldesrhip
J.W. McGarvey

McGarvey's brief but thorough study on the eldership, focusing on the work that the shepherds of God's flock need to be doing. While he also discusses theological matters, this is an eminently practical work.

Original Commentary on Acts
J.W. McGarvey

McGarvey's classic commentary on Acts, attractively re-typeset and added to our Heritage of Faith collection.

Coming Soon
Natural Theology
William Paley

DeWard Original Publications

Beneath the Cross: *Essays and Reflections on the Lord's Supper*
Jady S. Copeland and Nathan Ward (editors)

The Lord's Supper is rich with meaning supplied
by Old Testament foreshadowing and New Testament teaching. Explore the depths of symbolism
and meaning found in the last hours of the Lord's
life in *Beneath the Cross*. Filled with short essays by
preachers, scholars, and other Christians, this book
is an excellent tool for preparing meaningful Lord's
Supper thoughts—or simply for personal study and
meditation. 329 pages. $14.99 (PB); $23.99 (HB).

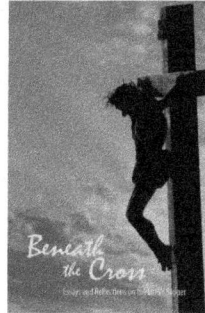

The Growth of the Seed: Notes on the Book of Genesis
Nathan Ward
A study of the book of Genesis that emphasizes two primary themes:
the development of the Messianic line and the growing enmity between
the righteous and the wicked. In addition, it provides detailed comments on the text and short essays on several subjects that are suggested
in, yet peripheral to, Genesis. 537 pages. $19.99.

The Big Picture of the Bible
Kenneth W. Craig
In this short book, the author summarizes the central theme of the
Bible in a simple, yet comprehensive approach. Evangelists across the
world have used this presentation to convert countless souls to the dis-
cipleship of Jesus Christ. Bulk discounts will be available, as will special
pricing for congregational orders. 48 pages, color. $4.99.

Boot Camp: Equipping Men with Integrity for Spiritual Warfare
Jason Hardin
According to Steve Arterburn, best-selling author of *Every Man's Battle,* "This is a great book to help us men live opposite of this world's
model of man." *Boot Camp* is the first volume in the IMAGE series of
books for men. It serves as a Basic Training manual in the spiritual war
for honor, integrity and a God-glorifying life. 237 pages, $13.99 (PB);
$24.99 (HB).

For a full listing of our titles, visit our website: www.dewardpublishing.com

DEWARD
PUBLISHING COMPANY